# Alexander the Great

The History and Legacy of the Macedonian King

*(How the Greatest Military Leader Expanded the Borders of the Known World)*

**Thomas Dugas**

Published By **Ryan Princeton**

# Thomas Dugas

All Rights Reserved

*Alexander the Great: The History and Legacy of the Macedonian King (How the Greatest Military Leader Expanded the Borders of the Known World)*

**ISBN 978-1-7775767-1-4**

No part of this guidebook shall be reproduced in any form without permission in writing from the publisher except in the case of brief quotations embodied in critical articles or reviews.

Legal & Disclaimer

The information contained in this book is not designed to replace or take the place of any form of medicine or professional medical advice. The information in this book has been provided for educational & entertainment purposes only.

The information contained in this book has been compiled from sources deemed reliable, and it is accurate to the best of the Author's knowledge; however, the Author cannot guarantee its accuracy and validity and cannot be held liable for any errors or omissions. Changes are periodically made to this book. You must consult your doctor or get professional medical advice before using any of the suggested remedies, techniques, or information in this book.

Upon using the information contained in this book, you agree to hold harmless the Author from and against any damages, costs, and expenses, including any legal fees potentially resulting from the application of any of the information provided by this guide. This disclaimer applies to any damages or injury caused by the use and application, whether directly or indirectly, of any advice or information presented, whether for breach of contract, tort, negligence, personal injury, criminal intent, or under any other cause of action.

You agree to accept all risks of using the information presented inside this book. You need to consult a professional medical practitioner in order to ensure you are both able and healthy enough to participate in this program.

## Table Of Contents

Chapter 1: Early Life and Background ...... 1

Chapter 2: Rise to Power ...... 14

Chapter 3: The Persian Campaigns ......... 26

Chapter 4: Expansion to the East .......... 43

Chapter 5: Personal Life and Character .. 56

Chapter 6: The Death of Alexander ........ 67

Chapter 7: The Dawn of Greatness ........ 75

Chapter 8: The Ascend to Power ........... 79

Chapter 9: Unifying Greece .................... 84

Chapter 10: The Persian Wars ................ 88

Chapter 11: The Conqueror of Worlds ... 93

Chapter 12: The Price of Power ............. 97

Chapter 13: Personal Life of a Legend .. 101

Chapter 14: "The Downfall" .................. 105

Chapter 15: The Legacy ....................... 109

Chapter 16: Alexander and Us ............. 114

Chapter 17: Alexander ........................ 118

Chapter 18: Alexander's leadership ..... 132

Chapter 19: Individual sacrifices .......... 152

Chapter 20: Alexander's desire to drink 161

Chapter 21: Determination .................. 176

## Chapter 1: Early Life and Background

The lineage and birth of Alexander the Great

Alexander the Great, the famous conqueror of the old world was born in the year 356 BCE in the kingdom of ancient times of Macedonia. He was the son of King Philip II of Macedon and Queen Olympias. The birthplace of his father was in the capital of Pella which is located in the northern part of Greece. The birth of Pella marked the start of a fascinating trip that would alter the geography of the world in antiquity.

Alexander's genealogy can be traced back to the bloodlines of royalty in Macedonia. His grandfather the king, Philip II was well-known for his military savvy and strategic plan that allowed his reign to unite the conflicting Greek cities under Macedonian government. Philip's reign witnessed the growth and consolidating of Macedonian power, and laid the foundation for the future victories of his son.

From his maternal side, Alexander has a link with the ancient Greek the hero Achilles. Olympias believed that he was directly descendent from Achilles and considered him to be her ancestral ancestor. The lineage added to the mythology around Alexander's birth, and inspired his aspirations to the highest level.

Alexander's early life was influenced by prominent people throughout his life. One of his major teachers was the famous philosopher Aristotle whom he personally taught his students in many areas such as literature, philosophy and even sciences. With the guidance of Aristotle, Alexander was able to develop a passion for education and a respect of Greek theology and culture and philosophy, which would significantly influence his views on the world and actions to come.

Alexander was a young man. Alexander had exceptional characteristics from the beginning of his life. He had an unstoppable interest as well as a ferocious drive as well as a desire for knowledge and excitement. The early introduction to the his life in the royal court and combat operations led by his father, instilled an in-depth respect for strategy in the army as well as leadership.

When he was just 16, Alexander received a taste of authority and accountability as he was appointed the regent of Macedonia even though his father was in a war. It was a chance for him to prove his leadership qualities as well as gain invaluable insights on the process of governance and the decision-making process.

Unfortunately, the childhood of Alexander was not without conflict and strife within the family. The turbulent relationships between his parents together with the competitive characteristics that was the Macedonian court led to a culture rife with intrigue in the political realm and power battles. Alexander's conflicting relationship with his parents ultimately caused their separation, and the deportation of the queen Olympias.

As Alexander got older, he was more aware of his personal future and the legacy it was his destiny to leave to his children. Alexander was motivated by the determination to exceed the accomplishments of his father, and to make his own name that would be heard throughout into the future.

The history of the birth and lineage of Alexander the Great established the basis for his extraordinary journey of victory and helped shape his dreams to achieve greatness. From his princely Macedonian family heritage, to his growing up under the direction of Aristotle and the Aristotle family, these influencers played an important part in shaping the prince's young mind into a visionary, ambitious leader, who left an imprint on the history of ancient civilizations.

Childhood and Education Under Aristotle

Alexander the Great's youth and his education, under the guidance of the famous philosopher Aristotle had a crucial impact on his as well as cultural development. At an early age, Alexander exhibited exceptional potential and was given Aristotle's guidance, which marked the start of an era of development that will greatly impact his later successes.

Being the prince of Alexander, the son of King Philip II of Macedon and the Queen of Olympias, Alexander was born to a world filled with conflict and intrigue in the world of politics as well as military ambition. From the beginning of his life his natural interest and a desire to study, which attracted all those who knew him. In recognition of his talent and potential, his parents pushed for an education that was the most effective to him, and Alexander was put under the supervision of Aristotle who was one of the best philosophy experts of his time.

Aristotle who was one of the Plato pupil, became famous for his broad understanding and intellect. Alexander's training under Aristotle was a long period in which he was taught in a myriad of disciplines, including the sciences, literature, philosophy and rhetoric. The teachings of Aristotle profoundly affected Alexander's outlook on life, imparting to his a profound love of Greek theology, philosophy as well as intellectual pursuits.

With the guidance of Aristotle, Alexander acquired a solid basis in science and the arts and honed critical thinking as well as the capacity to think critically about difficult issues. Aristotle advocated a comprehensive method of education and encouraged students to study various fields of study and gain a greater knowledge about the universe. The multidisciplinary approach to education will later be instrumental for Alexander's military operations and in his ability to manage different civilizations.

The training Alexander received went far beyond the realm of his theoretical knowledge. Aristotle believed in the value in physical development and encouraged in Alexander an interest in athletic fitness as well as military training. The philosopher introduced Alexander to the writings of Homer and particularly to his epic work The Iliad, which recounted the epic actions of heroes such as Achilles. The Iliad inspired Alexander's love of noble ideals, and later became an inspiration source for his dreams.

As Alexander got older, his educational pursuits expanded beyond the the class. He was a part of his father's battles in the military, getting first-hand experiences in the field of military strategy as well as the leadership. Being exposed to the challenges of battle further sharpened his tactical thinking skills and helped develop an appreciation for camaraderie among his fellow soldiers.

The influence of Aristotle extended far beyond his intellectual activities. Aristotle also imparted moral and ethical principles to Alexander and stressed how important it was to be virtuous as well as temperance. These lessons set the stage to Alexander's sense of respect and a commitment to lead through example.

The knowledge offered by Aristotle helped to create the distinctive combination of intellect as well as cultural understanding and strategic thought that shaped Alexander's personality. The school fueled his ambitions and inspired his military efforts and helped shape his idea of a common empire that merged Greek and Eastern cultural traditions.

While Alexander's time under Aristotle came to an end when he was crowned the throne upon his father's murder however, the influence of his studies remained in his life. The principles and teachings taught by Aristotle provided a direction factor, influencing his decisions and shaping his interaction with different cultures when Alexander embarked on his great victories.

The early years and the education of Alexander The Great, who was the son of Aristotle established the foundation for his remarkable accomplishments. The experience gave him the intellectual skills, the cultural understanding as well as the ability to think strategically to be one of the world's best military leaders and to be a constant image of ambition and interest.

The relationship with his father, His Relationship with His Father, Philip II

Alexander the Great's friendship with his father the King Philip II of Macedon, had a significant impact on shaping his character, aspirations and ultimately his success in his rise to the throne. The relationship between the father and son was deep and varied, characterized by the rivalry of both sides, as well as influence.

The king Philip II was an impressive individual He was renowned for his military savvy and political savvy. Philip II transformed Macedonia from a modest kingdom to a major power within the ancient Greece and laid the groundwork for Alexander's subsequent victories. When he was a prince in his youth, Alexander saw his father's successes in the military as well as the unification between the Greek city-states as well as subjugation of regions that were rebellious.

Philip was aware of the potential in his son and set out to prepare him for the challenge of being a ruler. He sought the assistance of famous tutors, such as philosopher Aristotle and the philosopher Aristotle, to provide Alexander with a thorough training. Philip's choice to put Alexander under the direction of these renowned teachers proved the dedication to shaping Alexander into a competent and rounded administrator.

Although they shared the same goals, Alexander's relationships with his father wasn't with no tension. As Alexander got older and his prowess in the military began to be apparent, he developed an awareness of his future as well as a determination to beat the achievements of his father. The ambition sometimes squabbled with Philip's ambitions and his desire to rule the realm.

The conflict between the father and son was brought into the spotlight as Philip married again and was blessed with the name of Arrhidaeus. The new heir could threaten Alexander's standing as the heir of the throne. But, fate intervened and Alexander's place was secure by the time Arrhidaeus was found to be ineligible to govern due to an impairment in his mental state.

The bond that binds Alexander Philip and Alexander Philip was further tested during an encounter against the Illyrians. Alexander was the regent during the absence of his father and able to lead a successful battle that demonstrated his ability to think strategically. The victory strengthened Alexander's standing as a competent leader, and raised his status within the Macedonian nobles.

Tragically, prior to the father and son were able to fully reach a consensus and fulfill their mutual goals, King Philip II was assassinated in 336 BCE. The reasons for his death remain a mystery and it did mark an important turning point in Alexander's story. He was just 20 years old when he He ascended the throne and assumed position of the king, and inherited the work of his father that was not completed and hopes.

Philip's influence on Alexander was indisputable however, his death was also allowed Alexander from potential limitations or conflicts. Since he was the sole leader in Macedonia, Alexander could now achieve his goals in a large scale free of the pressure to be competitive or seeking the approval of his father.

Over the next several years, Alexander is a hero in his combats in the military, capturing vast regions and building an empire that stretches across Greece up to Egypt as well as India. In spite of his father's absence Philip's legacy loomed huge providing the source of inspiration as well as an indicator by the which Alexander evaluated his successes.

The connection with Alexander the Great and his father Philip II, the King Philip II, was a multifaceted mix of love competition, respect, and power. Although tensions and uncertainty shaped the relationship, Philip's direction in military success, as well as the untimely passing of his son were key elements in determining Alexander's personality as well as his ambitions and final path as one of the most formidable warriors.

## Chapter 2: Rise to Power

The accession of the King's throne

The tragic assassination of the king Philip II of Macedon in 336 BCE was a pivotal moment in the history of his son Alexander. When he was 20, Alexander became king and had to face the daunting responsibility of taking on the duties of the kingship. The moment of historical significance was the start of Alexander the Great's extraordinary experience as one of most powerful figures of ancient historical.

Alexander's claim on the throne initially questioned upon his father's passing; certain sections in the Macedonian court doubted his ability to lead and tried to undermine his authority. But, Alexander quickly took decisive steps to ensure his place as the legitimate monarch of Macedon. With the help of faithful commandos and prominent leaders, Alexander swiftly removed potential adversaries and strengthened his position.

In order to consolidate his position, Alexander tried to earn the trust and respect of his fellow members of the Macedonian elite and his army. Alexander portrayed himself as an appropriate successor to the legacy of his father by highlighting his strength in the military and charismatic leadership skills. Through a string of victories in military operations, Alexander demonstrated his strategic excellence and gained his admiration and the respect of his troops.

The initial test for Alexander's leadership occurred in the year 335 BCE when Alexander began a war against the city-states rebelling in Greece This operation, also known as the Hellenic League, aimed to establish Macedonian supremacy over Greek city-states as well as avenge prior violations towards his dad. With the help of negotiation and power, Alexander successfully subdued the oppositional factions, strengthening his power over Greece and making himself an effective commander.

In the midst of having Greece under the control of Alexander, Alexander turned his attention towards the east and set an eye on the massive Persian Empire. Motivated by his father's dreams of taking revenge on the Persian invasion of Greece and motivated by his own goals, Alexander set off on a number of wars which would see him come face-to-face with Darius III, the Persian King Darius III.

The year the 334th year BCE, Alexander crossed the Hellespont The narrow strait between Europe and Asia and Asia, accompanied by the aid of 40 000 soldiers. The bold move of Alexander was the start of his infamous Persian campaign, also known in the Wars of Alexander the Great. The subsequent battles and culminated in the victories decisive in Granicus, Issus, and Gaugamela will alter the landscape of geopolitics in the early world.

Alexander's successes in the military and the ability to inspire an unwavering devotion from his soldiers established his status as an admired leader. Alexander's victories over enemies and the establishment of an empire that extended all the way from Greece up to Egypt and as far as India gave him the name "the Great" and cemented his position in history.

The crowning of Alexander the Great brought about a major change for Alexander's reign. From the challenges in securing his kingly position and pursuing the most ambitious of military campaigns Alexander demonstrated extraordinary leadership as well as strategic thinking and a unwavering commitment to live up to his potential. The following years saw him become one of the most renowned military wizards, leaving his mark in the history of our world, and setting the history of generations to come.

Consolidation of Power Within Macedonia

Consolidation of power within Macedonia was an important move in the life of Alexander the Great when he was elevated into the position of king. After inheriting a kingdom that expanded under the reign of his father Philip II, the King Philip II. Alexander was faced with the task to maintain stability while asserting his authority across an expansive and varied realm. By combining political moves, military operations and strategic alliances Alexander was able to consolidate his position in Macedonia and established his status as the supreme head of the kingdom.

Alexander's initial task was to gain the trust and trust of the Macedonian nobles. This was vital to assure that they accepted his reign as king as well as to prevent potential opposition against his authority. Alexander honored loyal patrons by granting title and position of influence and also incorporated trustworthy individuals to his circle of friends. Through the cultivation of a network followers and rewarding those who were loyal He established a solid position of power in the realm.

Alexander Also, he took steps to put down rebellions or discord in order to strengthen his position. He was decisive in dealing with revolts and threats that could arise, speedily getting rid of rivals and dissident groups. Alexander's standing as a powerful military commander was essential to deterring potential challengers as Alexander proved his power and determination in executing success in his military campaigns as well as successful strategic wins.

Alexander recognized the significance to maintain control over important regions in Macedonia. Alexander strategically put the most trusted administrators and commanders strategically in key positions to ensure that these regions' trust as well as efficient administration. Through delegating authority to competent people and ensuring that they had a close watch the administration that offered security and efficient administration for his kingdom.

As well as securing trust to the Macedonian nobility, and keeping the control of key areas, Alexander also sought to increase his influence through unions and marriages. He was able to marry noblewomen of influential families. This included Roxana who was the daughter of an influential Bactrian nobleman and Stateira her daughter, who was Darius III, the defeated Persian Darius III. Darius III. The marriages strengthened his political ties and showed his determination to bring diverse cultures together in his empire.

Alexander was also able to implement administrative reforms that streamlined administration and ensure centralized control. Alexander established a system of the satrapies. Governors were appointed as satraps, who were entrusted with the oversight of local matters as well as take care of tax collection. He was able to keep an authoritative central government and delegate certain duties to trusted persons.

Additionally, Alexander's successes in the military contributed to strengthening the power of Macedonia. The conquests and expansion of the empire brought immense riches and resources that were utilized to reward his loyal followers and increase his power. The war spoils such as vast treasures and areas, added to his power and prestige.

Alexander the Great was able to consolidate power in Macedonia with his political acumen and military skill, as well as strategic alliances, as well as effective management. His capacity to navigate complicated political environments, subdue internal conflict, and retain dominance over important regions was a key factor to his continued rule as one of the world's most powerful leaders. His consolidation of power in Macedonia was an important step that allowed the Macedonians to pursue their ambitious goals of capturing the Persian Empire as well as shaping the direction of history from ancient times.

Conquests in Greece

Alexander the Great's victories over Greece was a key aspect of his initial battles and played a major part in the establishment of his power and growing the scope of his empire. As he ascended to the throne of the year 336 BCE, Alexander swiftly turned to establishing supremacy on the Greek city-states which was historically fragmented and sometimes in conflict to Macedonian rule.

One of the main goals of Alexander's campaign throughout Greece was to increase the power of his empire and to assert his legitimacy as the son to his father Philip II. Philip II. Even though Philip had succeeded in uniting a lot of Greece under Macedonian dominance but there were some pockets of discontent and simmering tensions between cities-states in particular.

To accomplish his goals, Alexander employed a combination of military force, diplomacy and strategic alliances. Alexander sought to influence the Greek city-states with diplomatic persuasiveness, highlighting his

Hellenic tradition and positioning his self as an advocate of Greek liberty and culture. He sought to frame his administration as an extension of the policies of his father and highlighting the advantages of Macedonian management and the stability.

In 336 BCE After assuming the throne Alexander had to face a threat immediately from Thebes an influential city-state determined to free itself from Macedonian dominance. As a response, Alexander swiftly marched his troops to Thebes to thwart the uprising and defeated the city. Then, he set an example for future rebellions to avoid.

The devastating defeat at Thebes delivered a powerful message to Greek cities-states: Alexander determinedly fought to keep Macedonian dominance. A number of city-states, conscious of the futility of fighting decided to bow to Alexander's authority to avoid the repercussions. Some, who were aware of the strength of his army, to join his cause seeing Alexander as a man who would protect their interests as well as provide stability.

The Battle of Chaeronea in 338 BCE was an important pivotal moment in Alexander's victory of Greece. As the commander of the combined Macedonian and Greek troops, Alexander decisively beat the armies of his allies from Athens and Thebes giving him a firm grip over the area. In the aftermath of the battle Alexander was gracious and mercy-filled, pardoning several wounded Greek soldiers. This further demonstrated his determination to unify Greece under his control.

Alexander established his League of Corinth in 337 BCE following his victory at Chaeronea. The gathering brought together officials of various Greek cities, and under Alexander's direction the members pledged loyalty to him as supreme ruler of Greece. The League served as an unifying factor, and was instrumental in promoting the cooperation and defense of the Greek states, and also recognizing Alexander's power.

Once he had secured his spot having secured his position in Greece, Alexander set his goals to conquer more massive territories to the east, most notably in the Persian Empire. The victories he won in Greece set the stage for the subsequent expeditions to war and gave him the funds, resources, as well as the reputation needed for the ambitious plans he had.

Alexander's defeats in Greece were a major impact. They strengthened his authority over the region, and made him a revered diplomatic and military leader. The Greek city-states, which were previously separated, are now recognizing their legitimacy and played an integral part in the subsequent defeats, supplying forces, materials, and the political backing.

## Chapter 3: The Persian Campaigns

Motives for Invading Persia

Alexander the Great's incursion into Persia was fueled by a mixture of political, personal and strategic motivations. An urge to get revenge the pursuit of glory and fame, as well as a belief of the historical future, as well as strategically-oriented considerations drove his choice to go on the massive campaign.

One of the main reasons Alexander invaded Persia was revenge for the earlier Persian attacks on Greece. In the Persian Empire, which was under the reign of monarchs like Darius I and Xerxes I and Xerxes I, launched numerous combats against Greece at the end of the early 5th century BCE and included the famous Persian Wars. These wars have profoundly impacted Greek society and its culture. Alexander considered himself to be the defender of Greek liberty and wanted to repay these embarrassing experiences by fighting towards the lands of Persia.

A further reason for Alexander was his pursuit of self-esteem and glory. Alexander was profoundly inspired by the epic tales of Achilles and the mythical Greek fighter from The Trojan War, and sought to be better than his achievements. Alexander was motivated by a strong determination to make a impression on the history of mankind and be regarded as a conqueror and a ruler that was more successful than all the others that came before his time. The victory over the powerful Persian Empire, famous for its power and wealth, enabled him to attain unparalleled recognition and glory.

Alexander thought in his destiny to take on his own Persian Empire. He viewed himself as a symbol of divine favour and thought that gods had chosen for him to accomplish a great task. His conquests were an opportunity to bring Greek civilization and culture to all of the globe, establishing a world empire which would unify both the East as well as the West.

Strategically, the invasion of Persia offered Alexander with numerous advantages. It was a vast and prosperous empire. Persian Empire was large and prosperous, with plenty of sources of resources as well as opportunities to expand. Its strategically placed location bridged East and West, providing the gateway for further conquers within Central Asia and India. In control of Persia will provide Alexander with an enormous geopolitical power and economic strength.

In addition the internal dynamics within the Persian Empire were a factor in the motivation for Alexander's invasion. The Empire was plagued by disputes over succession as well as internal conflicts, which created the occasion for Alexander to take advantage of the weak points and conflicts in his own Persian court. Through leveraging these internal battles and aiming to overthrow the Persian monarchy and make himself the next ruler. He brought peace and stability under his reign.

As a summary, Alexander the Great's reasons for launching an invasion of Persia were multifaceted. These included the desire to take revenge for his previous Persian invaders in Greece as well as a desire for fame and glory as well as a belief in history's destiny, and also the strategic aspects that interacted with his dream and ambition of building a massive empire. All of these reasons drove him to take on an incredibly daring combats of the military in all history.

Battles and Victories in Anatolia

Battles and Victories in Anatolia: Alexander the Great's Conquest

Anatolia The region that is part of the present-day Turkey was a key contribution to Alexander the Great's military operations and in his struggle to defeat the Persian Empire. Within Anatolia, Alexander faced formidable enemies, took on fierce battles and won important victories which helped to build his status as an outstanding strategic military leader and strengthened his authority over the area.

One of the earliest major battles that took place in Anatolia occurred during that of the Battle of the Granicus River in 334 BCE. In 334 BCE, as Alexander moved eastward and fought against the Persian army headed by Memnon from Rhodes. Memnon of Rhodes was the commander. Persians tried to stop his progress and secure their territories to the west. Although they were defeated, Alexander skillfully deployed his forces and employed innovative tactics to defeat the Persian opposition. Through his superior discipline and the cavalry's charges, Alexander emerged victorious, beating the Persians as well as gaining control over the western part of Anatolia.

After following the Battle of the Granicus, Alexander was able to move towards the west facing several cities as well as areas who resisted the rule of his father. One of them cities was Halicarnassus which he fought fierce resistance from the defense forces. It was the Siege of Halicarnassus which took place in 334 BCE demonstrated Alexander's strategic savvy and determination. Following a long siege his troops smashed through the walls of the city, seizing the city, and then firmly established Macedonian dominance over the area.

In the midst of his battle continuing his campaign Anatolia, Alexander faced his most formidable adversary to date in 333 BCE. The Persian Darius III. Darius III. Darius III's Battle of Issus is a crucial moment in the battles of Alexander. In command of a huge Persian military, Darius hoped to crush the Macedonian army and stop the expansion of their army to the east. Alexander's exceptional tactical skills and boldness allowed Alexander to defeat the Persians and win victory. Darius III's defeat Darius III at Issus shattered Persian confidence, and helped Alexander to strengthen his grip over Anatolia even more.

Following following the Battle of Issus, Alexander turned his sights to the strategically important city of Gordium located in central Anatolia. In this city, he famously came across the Gordian Knot. It was a complicated knot that was tied by the antiquated King Gordius. The legend said that anyone who managed to tie the knot was destined to rule over all of Asia. With a powerful and symbolic gesture, Alexander, unable to tie the knot again, took his sword, and cut it. This demonstrated his determination and determination to be the king of Asia.

In the year 333 BCE Alexander began his march towards the east, engaging in more fights while subduing the resistance in the process. It was the Battle of Gaugamela fought in 331 BCE was the culmination of Alexander's Anatolian campaign. In the face of Darius III once again, Alexander used a variety of strategic tactics and the disciplined military to take on the Persians. The victory of Gaugamela proved to be a devastating loss against the Persian Empire and resulted in the abolition of their troops as well as the capture of Darius III.

The wars and victories of Anatolia was crucial to Alexander's victory in the overall battle against his Persian Empire. In these battles, Alexander displayed his strength in battle in his adaptability and capability to inspire loyalty and trust to his soldiers. These victories in Anatolia helped secure Macedonian dominance over the area and provided a strong foundation that Alexander could pursue his expansion into the east and realize his dream of capturing the Persian center.

Apart from its military importance and importance, Alexander's conquers of Anatolia have had significant cultural and geopolitical consequences. The integration of Anatolia to the empire of Alexander was a significant event that brought Greek influence as well as Hellenistic cultural influence to the region that encouraged the integration of cultures and leaving an imprint which would influence the course of time.

The victories and battles that took place in Anatolia represented important milestones during Alexander the Great's victories and exemplifying his military genius as well as his unstoppable determination to be a leader.

Siege of Tyre and Conquest of Egypt The Siege of Tyre and the conquer of Egypt were two major battles that Alexander the Great undertook during his Persian Empire conquest. These victories showed his strategic ability, determination and capability to over come massive obstacles on his way to for dominance.

The Siege of Tyre (332 BCE): Tyre, located in the middle of an island off the coast of modern-day Lebanon it was a strong and fortified city that was able to withstand previous attacks. The strategic location and robust defenses created a powerful obstruction to Alexander's army. But, Alexander was determined to defeat Tyre in order to gain dominance over the east of the Mediterranean.

Alexander initially tried to reach a deal with Tyre and sought access to the city as well as its resources. But Tyre's Tyrians were confident of their securing position, refused Alexander's demands. Unfazed, Alexander devised an audacious strategy to thwart the city's defences.

He commissioned the construction of a causeway or mole, connecting the mainland towards Tyre's island. Tyre. The feat of engineering was monumental and involved the transport of stone as well as rubble and timber to build a land bridge. In spite of constant opposition from the Tyrians and military attacks and set fire at the causeway army were able to hold their ground.

After the causeway had been completed, Alexander launched a full-scale attack on the city. The army smashed the walls as his navy blocked Tyre by cutting off its transportation lines to the sea. After months of fierce fighting, Alexander's troops pierced the city's walls, and took Tyre. The remaining Tyrians who had sought refuge in the temples of the city were sold into slavery and the city was slain by destruction and plunder.

The victory over Tyre was an important victory for Alexander who demonstrated his capability to conquer seemingly impossible obstacles as well as securing his dominance over the east Mediterranean coast.

The Conquest of Egypt (332-331 BCE): Following the fall of Tyre, Alexander turned his sights on Egypt and it was under Persian authority. The Egyptians were dissatisfied by Persian rule were delighted to welcome Alexander to be a liberator and they welcomed him by a warm welcome when he arrived.

At Memphis, Alexander was proclaimed as the Pharaoh of Egypt and further strengthened his power and positioning his self as the legitimate successor to the previous Egyptian rulers. Alexander showed respect to Egyptian traditions and customs by visiting the temple of Amun-Ra in Siwa's Oasis of Siwa and receiving an oath of confirmation from God for his deity.

Alexander established Alexandria, the capital city. Alexandria and it would grow into the center of Hellenistic trade and culture throughout the years to come. Alexander also led a campaign of military force into the west of the Nile Delta to secure his authority over the region.

The victory over Egypt brought Alexander with a wealth of sources. Alexander took advantage of Egypt's fertile soils and plentiful grain reserves in the Nile to support his army and fund future military operations. His surrender to Egypt has also cut off Persian supplies lines weakening their control on the region.

These victories over Egypt were a major moment in the empire-building efforts of Alexander. The fertile landscapes of Egypt gave him a solid foundation of strength and also was a launching pad for his future goals which allowed him to strengthen his authority throughout the region, and to prepare for the next stage of his conquers.

The Siege of Tyre and the defeat of Egypt showed Alexander's determination, strategic skills and the ability to conquer massive difficulties. These victories also grew the empire of Alexander, secured crucial strategic positions and boosted the strength and resources of his troops and pushed him with his unstoppable march to take on his empire. Persian Empire.

Battle of Gaugamela and Fall of the Persian Empire

The Battle of Gaugamela fought in 331 BCE was an important conflict in the battle between Alexander the Great and Darius III of Persia. Darius III of Persia. The epic battle was the turning point of Alexander's battle and led to the fall of the powerful Persian Empire.

The context: At at the time that of Battle of Gaugamela, Alexander had already won significant victories over the Persians which included that of the Battle of Issus. But Darius III, the Persian ruler, was still leading the army of a great strength and aimed to thwart Alexander's advance.

Strategies and Preparations: Darius III assembled a large army of more than 200 000 soldiers, which included war elephants and cavalry. Contrarily, Alexander led a smaller but well-organized and battle-tough army of around 47,000 soldiers comprising infantry, cavalry and specific groups.

Conscient of the Persian advantages in numbers, Alexander devised a meticulous plan to defeat the Persian force. Alexander sought to capitalize on the weak points in Darius's strategy and utilize his greater mobility in cavalry, coordination, and mobility in order to gain victory.

The Battle: When the battle began, Darius deployed his chariots and scythed chariots with the hope to dismantle his Macedonian formation. Alexander's army were able to evade the attack of chariots and rendered them useless. Alexander later led a ferocious cavalry assault, specifically targeting Darius.

The Macedonian phalanx continued to advance steadily as it was the Companion Cavalry, led by Alexander was engaged in a intense battle against the Persian cavalry. The Macedonian troops' superior military in training, discipline, and unity proved crucial as they slowly gained an advantage in the war.

Despite Darius's efforts to unite his army, Persian lines were beginning to fall due to the constant pressure exerted by Alexander's troops. Fearing defeat, Darius fled the battlefield with his troops, and the army was left without leaders and scattered.

The outcome and the fall of the Persian Empire: The Battle of Gaugamela was a huge triumph for Alexander. The Persian loss was significant however, the Macedonians had comparatively small losses. The victory provided the opportunity for Alexander to enter the middle of the Persian Empire and take control.

After the battle the battle of Gaugamela, Alexander pursued Darius but was subsequently killed and betrayed by commanding officers. Once Darius gone, Alexander declared himself the proper leader over the Persian Empire, and continued his conquers.

Alexander's next campaigns took the city to Babylon, Susa, and Persepolis that fell under Alexander's control. There was sporadic resistance from Persian forces, and embarked upon combat missions to contain revolts. Through time the empire of Alexander grew to cover areas that once were considered to be part of the Persian Empire and marked the end of Persian rule in the region.

The Battle of Gaugamela and the following end of the Persian Empire represented a crucial moment in the history of the world. Alexander's victories triggered the shift in culture and politics called the Hellenistic period. It expanded Greek influence throughout the territories conquered and had an impact that lasted for centuries on design, art, philosophy as well as governance.

The Battle of Gaugamela was pivotal to Alexander's war to defeat the Persian Empire. With his tactical genius as well as his savvy tactics and a unwavering commitment of his troops, Alexander achieved a decisive victory. This led to the demise of the Persian Empire, and the emergence of his vast empire, which extended across Greece up to Egypt, Persia, and beyond.

## Chapter 4: Expansion to the East

Conquest of Bactria and Sogdiana

The conquer of Bactria and Sogdiana by Alexander the Great was a crucial moment of his arduous battles in the East. The regions of Bactria and Sogdiana, which are located in the present-day Afghanistan, Uzbekistan, and Tajikistan were a unique set of challenges and opportunities to Alexander in his quest to increase his power and consolidate his authority over the vast areas which he had defeated.

Bactria is located northwest of the Hindu Kush mountain range, was a region that was once renowned for its abundance of resources which included fertile lands, important minerals and skilled artisans. In the northern part of Bactria, Sogdiana was inhabited by the Sogdians the Persian-speaking population famous for their trade and commercial activities on the Silk Road. Both areas were strategically important because of their geographic position which served as important trade routes linking both the East as well as the West.

Alexander's conquer of Bactria and Sogdiana started in 329 BCE in the wake of his defeat against Darius III, the Persian King Darius III and the capture of Persepolis, the Persian capital city, Persepolis. In his quest to conquer the east the Persian Empire faced fierce opposition by local rulers, as well as rocky terrains. This included the formidable Central Asia mountains as well as brutal deserts.

The battle for Bactria, Alexander faced resistance from the local ruler Bessus who had declared himself as the rightful succeeding ruler to Darius III. Although he faced initial difficulties and was a victim of the tactics of guerilla warfare employed by the Bactrians Alexander's military savvy and the devotion of his troops enabled him to conquer these obstacles. Alexander was able to capture Bessus and quickly incorporated Bactria to his growing empire.

Sogdiana But, the Sogdiana presented an additional challenge to Alexander. Sogdians are known for their tenacity and ferocious fight, fought hard to defend their homelands against the invaders of the Macedonian army. Cities like Samarkand as well as Marakanda (modern-day Samarkand and Shahrisabz and Shahrisabz, respectively) were major battlefields.

A ferocious battle, a brutal siege and tactical maneuvering defined Alexander's battle in Sogdiana. He used both forces and diplomatic techniques in order to control the Sogdians. In certain instances the king granted amnesty for local officials who accepted his authority, while at other times, he turned to violence to stifle opposition. The iconic Siege of Sogdian Rock stands in the light as an example of the strength and determination shown by Alexander when it came to overcoming fortifications that appeared impervious.

Even with the odds Alexander's military skills and determination finally helped him conquer

Bactria as well as Sogdiana. The victories granted him the control of important trade routes as well as access to precious resources, increasing the power of his empire's economy and power. He set up regional post-military and administrative outposts to ensure his power and influence could be recognized.

Additionally, Alexander recognized the importance in integrating local people within his empire. Alexander implemented a system of fusion and encouraged intermarrying between his Macedonian soldiers and the local population. The goal was to encourage an integration between cultures and to reduce tensions between conquerors and those who were conquered.

The conquer of Bactria and Sogdiana showed Alexander's unwavering in pursuit of his Eastern goals. These victories established his dominance over the huge territories that stretched across Greece through the middle of Asia creating an empire that spanned east and west. In addition, the victories in these regions paved the way for further missions into India as a testament to his steadfast commitment and determination to create an enormous, united empire.

Crossing the Hindu Kush and Reaching India

The crossing of across the Hindu Kush Mountain range and getting to India was a major and difficult feat achieved through Alexander the Great in the course of his wars throughout the East. It was a huge and difficult feat. Hindu Kush, a formidable mountain that ran through present-day Afghanistan as well as Pakistan was a formidable logistical and geographical difficulties. But Alexander's determination, strategy-oriented planning and the tenacity of his soldiers enabled them to overcome this difficult terrain, and finally enter the Indian subcontinent.

The journey across the Hindu Kush started around 329 BCE when Alexander was leading his army from Bactria to the region of mountains. The rough terrain, the extreme temperatures, and the absence of routes that were established presented significant obstacles. The Macedonian army was faced with dangerous mountains as well as deep gorges and mountain cliffs with steep sides, which made their progress slow and painful. They were required to travel through small spaces, endure the harsh winters, and deal with shortages of resources.

In order to overcome the obstacles, Alexander employed careful planning as well as local guides who had a thorough understanding of the mountains. He instructed his engineers to build bridges, roads as well as makeshift pathways to ease transport of troops and equipment. At times it was necessary the option of climbing or deviating around difficult parts of the mountain.

Despite his hardships Alexander's leadership as well as the constant determination of his troops enabled them to persevere. Alexander's personal story of perseverance and sharing the hardships of his soldiers earned him gratitude and respect. Alexander's capacity to motivate and motivate his soldiers through difficult times was vital in keeping their morale high.

When he was able to successfully cross through the Hindu Kush, Alexander's army crossed into the provinces in the east that were part of the Achaemenid Empire. This included the present-day regions of Pakistan and north India. In this region, Alexander encountered a variety of local kingdoms and rulers which each one with their unique culture and abilities.

Alexander's early engagements in his first battles in the Indian subcontinent were characterized by victories in military battles against local kings like Porus who controlled the area of Punjab. It is the Battle of the Hydaspes River that took place in the year 326 BCE in which Alexander was confronted by a formidable adversary at the hands of Porus is regarded as a stunning accomplishment in the field of strategy for military and the ability to think strategically. Even though Alexander won the battle but the ferocious battle from Porus and his troops brought to light the obstacles he encountered when he fought his Indian battles.

When Alexander moved deeper into to the Indian subcontinent of India, the soldiers started to get tired. Long-running military operations and the unpredictability of the climate as well as the vastness of the Indian areas took a heavy strain on their morale as well as their physical wellbeing. In the face of a potential for further opposition from the formidable Indian monarchs and the troops tired, Alexander made the difficult choice of turning to the right.

Returning to the Hindu Kush proved just as demanding as the original crossing. The troops had to contend with extreme weather, supplies shortages, and battles with tribes that were hostile. In spite of these challenges, Alexander skillfully navigated his army back to safety through dangerous mountains, and returned to Bactria.

Although Alexander's Indian battles was not a permanent conquerors or an enduring Macedonian dominance over the area, it made a significant impression. Alexander's incursion to the Indian subcontinent was a catalyst for exchange of culture, trade and interactions between Greeks and Indians. This laid the foundation for the future interaction with East as well as West encouraging an understanding of one the other's cultures.

The crossing of across the Hindu Kush and finally reaching India demonstrated Alexander's determination dedication, determination, and military skills. This was a testament to his never-ending enthusiasm for adventure as well as the relentless pursuit of victory. While the Indian battle did not meet the goals of Alexander but it is a testimony to his courage as well as his permanent mark on history as one of the greatest conquerors.

Battles Against Porus and the Macedonian Army's Limits

The wars fought against the King Porus and the army of King Porus on the Indian subcontinent were among the most memorable and gruelling combats faced by Alexander the Great as well as his Macedonian soldiers. These wars, particularly that of Battle of the Hydaspes River proved the strength that the Macedonian army, and showed the strength to these Indian kingdoms.

The Battle of the Hydaspes River was fought in 326 BCE in the 326 BCE when Alexander's army moved further into India and came into contact with the King Porus who was the ruler of Punjab. Porus was a powerful Indian king, famous for his military skills and his formidable army of infantry, war elephants, and cavalry.

In the wake of previous Alexander's conquests and his military standing, Porus assembled a large army to protect his kingdom. The army was trained soldiers, backed by many war elephants, which are particularly terrifying to Macedonians that were inexperienced to battling such large beasts in battle.

In the course of battle, Porus and his forces showed great courage and grit. They stood firm against Macedonian attack, causing heavy losses and proved to be an imposing opponent. The elephants of war, particularly, presented an enormous challenge for the Macedonian phalanxes. They disrupted their lines of formation and creating anxiety among their troops.

Even in the beginning, despite problems however, the Macedonians under the direction of Alexander demonstrated their military skills and capability to adapt. Alexander came up with a plan to crush the elephants in war through a focus on the mahouts (handlers) and using precise attacks to cause chaos in the ranks of his adversaries. Furthermore, he exploited a gap within Porus the formation and launched targeted attacks to tear through the lines.

The fight was heatedly contested as both sides sustained major defeats. At the end of the day, the Macedonians won, however it came at an expensive cost. The Macedonian force was exhausted to its limit both mentally and physically. A long and exhausting battle, a new terrain, as well as their enemies' tenacity had taken an effect on their morale as well as their physical health.

The battle between Porus and his troops also highlighted the logistical problems facing the Macedonians on their journey across the Indian subcontinent. Long distances, uncertain climate and shortage of food and supplies strain their resources as well as challenged their capacity to carry on lengthy military campaigns. Additionally it was the case that Macedonian soldiers who had been on the run from their home for a long time were tired and longing to be able to return home to their homelands.

Due to the circumstances Alexander was forced to make the difficult choice to cut off his eastern expansion and return to Babylon. The wars fought against Porus revealed the limitations of Macedonian army's strength and endurance as well as the difficulty in conquering and managing large areas of India.

The interactions with Porus as well as other Indian kingdoms affected Alexander's understanding of the area and its strength in the military. Alexander was aware of the strength and power of Indian kingdoms, and was impressed by their military traditions. The recognition of this, along with his exhaustion in his troops as well as the logistical challenges, informed his choice to reorient his efforts towards consolidating his empire and encouraging the exchange of culture, rather than pursuing Eastward incursions.

## Chapter 5: Personal Life and Character

Relationships and Marriages

Marriages and relationships were a major factor in the lives of Alexander the Great. As a strong ruler who was also a diplomat, he made alliances, formed political partnership as well as joined marriages for strategically and for personal reasons. These alliances helped him increase his power, create important alliances, and promote the exchange of culture.

One of the more notable weddings during Alexander's lifetime was his marriage to Roxana an opulent woman in the region of Bactria. The ceremony occurred in the year 327 BCE when Alexander was fighting to the East. In marrying Roxana, Alexander sought to consolidate his power over areas he had conquered and gain his support from the nobility of the region. This alliance with Roxana was also instrumental in integrating the Persian nobility into the empire which promoted cultural integration and decreasing tensions between Macedonians and conquered populations.

Alongside Roxana, Alexander formed other important alliances in the politics of weddings. Alexander encouraged his generals as well as officers to marry local ladies and especially noble families. These unions created not only friendships but also assisted to create a sense of mutual interests and loyalty among his officers and commanders. Marriages between local women was part of Alexander's plan of fusion. His goal was to mix Greek and regional cultures for greater stability within his empire.

A significant part of Alexander's life was his intimate connection to Hephaestion, his close friend from childhood and his friend. Their bonds were such that it regularly resulted in speculation of the possibility of a connection. Hephaestion was a companion to Alexander during his battles as well as shared in his victories and difficulties, and held an influential position in the Empire. Their relationship was founded on trust, loyalty and respect for each other, Hephaestion acting as Alexander's trusted friend and adviser.

Alexander's relationship with his commanders and generals are also vital for the successful military campaigns he led. Alexander encouraged a sense of affection and camaraderie between his officers, and relied on their expertise and skills in executing his plans. They were treated as respected advisors and also delegated substantial tasks, which allowed them to be in charge of the areas they were assigned.

In addition, Alexander engaged in diplomatic weddings in order to strengthen his the political alliances of different ruling families. A notable instance is his wedding to Stateira his daughter Darius III, the Persian King he had defeated. The marriage was a sign of Alexander's determination to be recognized as an legitimate next king to succeed the Achaemenid Empire, and also to make a connection between his Greek as well as Persian worlds.

It's crucial to understand that, while Alexander had a number of weddings and relationships however his military ambitions and operations often predominated over matters of personal importance. Alexander spent most of his time in the absence of his wives and other loved ones as he led his troops in victories and expanding his empire. It led to tensions between his family and friends and, in certain instances there was political turmoil during his absence.

Leadership Style and Personality Traits

Alexander the Great's style of leadership and personal attributes played a major influence on his ability to inspire and command his troops to conquer huge areas, and leave an imprint in the history of the world. His distinctive blend of personality, power of speech and determination made him stand out as an outstanding leader.

One of Alexander's best-known characteristics as a leader was his charismatic, commanding presence. Alexander was a magnet which sparked loyalty and love to his soldiers. Alexander demonstrated his leadership by example constantly at the top of his unit when it was a combat, showing incredible courage and strength. The soldiers who fought alongside him admired his courage and unflinching commitment towards victory prompted them to fight for their lives with him.

Thinking strategically was another characteristic of Alexander's style of leadership. Alexander was a military-minded mentality, capable of understanding difficult situations and altering his tactics to suit. Alexander was never afraid to risk his life and think outside of the box. Alexander often used innovative strategies that caught adversaries out of their guards, which allowed him to win decisive battles. The ability to evaluate both the strength and weakness of his forces as well as his adversaries helped him take a sound decision on the field.

The determination and unwavering drive towards success were a major part of Alexander's character. Alexander was a man with an unquenchable desire to conquer and an unstoppable determination to achieve his goals. His uncompromising determination frequently pushed his physical and mental limits. physical and mental strength, inspiring the troops to follow his lead regardless of the daunting obstacles. Alexander's drive and determination to not concede defeat played a key part in his capacity to conquer obstacles and win incredible wins.

Although he was sometimes brutal in his attitude to war, Alexander also possessed a belief in fairness and justice. Alexander was renowned for showing the mercy of God to surrenderers to him, offering amnesty and averting their life. This strategy helped him win the trust and respect of the conquered population, since they believed that he was a kind and generous ruler, not a tyrant.

Alexander's leadership style was defined by his capacity to motivate and inspire his soldiers. Alexander had the knack of taking advantage of his troops' strengths and delegating responsibility to competent leaders, and encouraging an atmosphere of camaraderie within his soldiers. His soldiers were treated like comrades, and was concerned for their health, creating an unbreakable bond of trust and respect for each other.

But it's vital to recognize the fact that Alexander's style of leadership had its flaws. In his relentless pursuit of dominance, he often led to an indifference for the well-being of his soldiers and pushed them to their capabilities and subjecting the soldiers to risks that were not necessary. Furthermore, his egocentric nature and desire for fame occasionally led to tensions between his soldiers and led to a lack of respect.

Alexander's intellectual PursuitsAlexander Alexander the Great was an experienced general and passionate scholar with an ardent fascination with knowledge and the pursuit of learning. His pursuits in the realm of intellectuals profoundly shaped his style of management, and his ideas for the empire he wanted to create.

Alexander's greatest influencers in his mind was his teacher famous philosopher Aristotle. Aristotle was a tutor for Alexander in his youth and inspired him with a desire for learning and thirst for understanding. The guidance provided by Aristotle ensured that Alexander was educated on a range of topics, such as writing, philosophy, science and even political science. It gave him a solid knowledge base that informed his views on the world and government.

Alexander's curiosity for knowledge extended far beyond his formal studies. In his battles for the war Alexander was always seeking to learn about the culture and know-how of the nations which he fought. He was surrounded by philosophers, scholars and historians to create an atmosphere of intellectualism at the court of his. The scholars gave him invaluable insights into the customs practices, customs and philosophical tenets of the various peoples that were who were under his control.

Alexander began his an ambitious journey of exploration and scientific missions to discover new knowledge. Alexander gathered a group composed of scholars, scientists and geoscientists to accompany Alexander on his travels. These expeditions were designed to investigate and record the landscapes and flora, fauna as well as the cultures that he encountered on his journey. Alexander's curiosity for learning drove him to discover uncharted territory and to expand his the understanding of geography.

Additionally, Alexander had a deep love of literature and arts. Alexander carried around an original version of Iliad the ancient Greek epic poem that is believed to be written by Homer. The theme of heroics as well as glory and destiny were a common theme for Alexander and influenced his goals. Alexander also encouraged his development of libraries, and promoted the translation of literary works. He also helped facilitate the transfer of knowledge and ideas across various cultures.

Alexander's pursuit of knowledge influenced his philosophy of governance. Alexander sought to encourage the exchange of ideas and a fusion among the Greeks and conquered tribes and thereby fostering a sense of unification within the empire he ruled. He established cities which were centers for learning and encouraged interchange of ideas between various civilizations.

Furthermore, his intellectual interests led to his devotion to scholars as well as his support for intellectual debate. He aided philosophers financially, and was adamant that they participate in debates and intellectual discussions. This exchange of ideas allowed for diverse views to be heard, and also contributed to the growth of knowledge in his empire.

## Chapter 6: The Death of Alexander

Illness and Succession Plans

In the latter years of his time, Alexander the Great faced major health problems that profoundly impact his succession plans. This health issue and the absence of a clear successor created a sense of tension and uncertainty within his army, eventually creating the destiny of his empire upon the death of his father.

Alexander's health was beginning to deteriorate following years of constant battles and physical strain. In 323 BCE when he was at Babylon it was reported that he had fallen sick. The precise cause of his condition is an issue of contention among historians. Theories range between malaria, typhoid disease or even the possibility of poisoning. Whatever the reason, it's clear that his condition deteriorated quickly.

The news of Alexander's illness was reported, there was an unease in Alexander's generals as well as the Empire as a whole. Lack of a named successor exacerbated tensions, as different factions competed for influence and power. Alexander's inability to create an heir legitimate during his life left him without a source of authority and paved path for a potential succession crisis.

Due to the decline of his medical condition, Alexander was compelled to take on the question of succession. One of his final acts was to organize a large wedding, dubbed"the "Marriage of the Susa," where he was got married to a group of top-ranking Persian as well as Macedonian noblewomen. Their goal was to consolidate relationships in the realm of politics and to possibly create the legitimate heir to succeed to him.

Tragically, long before any concrete succession plan was ever implemented, Alexander passed away in the month of June in 323 BCE in the ripe aged of just 32. The sudden loss of his life caused his empire to fall into turmoil and ignited the power struggle between his generals. They were known as Diadochi, also known as successors.

While Alexander was absent, the generals first tried to preserve the unification of the empire, having agreed to govern collectively as well as protect Alexander's interests. But, the arrangement soon collapsed when ambitions fought and led to a string of battles between the Diadochi to defend their individual position of power.

Then, the empire of Alexander was divided into a number of successor kingdoms which saw his generals establish their own dynasties as well as ruling over various areas. The Hellenistic kingdoms, such as Macedon, the Seleucid Empire Ptolemaic Egypt as well as Macedon preserved Greek traditions and elements of administration and also took on local customs.

Lack of a clearly defined successor and an established succession plan led to the collapse of the empire Alexander ruled. Although he named his mentally handicapped halfbrother Arrhidaeus for his successor his choice was a source of contention but it was unable to stop the subsequent battles for power. In the absence of a main figure such as Alexander let his generals take control and influence the fate of their particular areas.

Controversies Surrounding His Death, Aftermath, and Division of His Empire

Following the demise of Alexander the Great in the year 323 BCE His vast empire had to endure a time of dramatic turmoil and discord. Without a clear successor, and an unfulfilled power gap in the top position the generals of his army, referred to as the Diadochi who fought for power, were involved in a battle to control power and those territories that he had defeated. The Aftermath of the death of Alexander resulted in the fragmentation of his empire into a number of Hellenistic kingdoms, each one governed by one of his generals, or their heirs.

The division of Alexander's Empire was initiated by the division of Babylon in the year 323 BCE which was the first time his generals decided to govern collectively to ensure the rights of his entire family. The arrangement was however uncertain, and conflict ensued as each general tried to strengthen their position and assert their dominance. Power struggles between the Diadochi caused a string of battles referred to by the name of Wars of the Diadochi or the Wars of the Successors.

The most notable and lasting successor states which emerged out of this division were:

1. It was the Seleucid Empire: Founded by Seleucus I Nicator who was among Alexander's best and most trusted generals The Seleucid Empire encompassed much of the old Persian areas, which includes present-day Iran, Iraq, Syria and the portions of Anatolia. The Seleucids built an imposing dynasty which had a monopoly on this large

region for a number of years, mixing Greek and Persian culture.

2. Ptolemaic Egypt: Ptolemy I Soter was another famous general, assumed the command of Egypt and established the Ptolemaic Dynasty. The Ptolemies were the rulers of Egypt for a period of nearly three centuries, creating an active Hellenistic tradition and becoming famous for their support of the science and the arts. Cleopatra was the final leader of the Ptolemaic Dynasty, is among of the most famous historical figures of the period.

3. It was the Antigonid Kingdom Antigonus I Monophthalmus one of the closest companions of Alexander was the founder of the Antigonid Kingdom that was centered around Macedonia as well as Greece. This dynasty was in control of Macedon over several generations but their influence diminished as time.

4. The Independent Greek City-States: A few Greek city-states, like Athens and Sparta have

regained their independence as well as maintained a certain measure of autonomy after Alexander's demise. Their strength and influence was greatly reduced compared to the glorious times of the ancient Greece.

These kingdoms that succeeded them, usually called the Hellenistic kingdoms, had a few elements of Greek cultural, administrative and language, while also incorporating parts of the conquered cultures. They established centralized government which encouraged trade and exchange, and encouraged spreading the Greek culture, language, and philosophy across their territory.

The dissolution of Alexander's empire and subsequent establishment of successor kingdoms have profound effects. The Hellenistic period saw the merging between Greek, Persian, and various other Eastern culture, resulting in an epoch of cosmopolitanism and vitality. The Hellenistic period also helped spread of Greek concepts and ideas throughout vast areas, adding to the development of science, philosophy as well as literature and artistic advances.

The division of the empire resulted in ongoing conflict and wars between the subsequent kingdoms. Power struggles persisted throughout the centuries, and included changing agreements, territorial dispute and even the intervention of foreign forces like Rome. Then, the encroaching Roman Empire gradually absorbed the Hellenistic kingdoms and marked the close of a period.

## Chapter 7: The Dawn of Greatness

In the middle of Macedonia in the midst of Macedonia's ancient past, surrounded by green hills and the peaceful water of the Aegean Sea. A young man who had a major destiny was born. Alexander who later became known by the name Alexander the Great was born into the world on the dazzling hot summer day in 356 BC. His father was King Philip II an imposing man with a strong determination and a formidable reputation as well as his mother queen Olympias she was a woman with deep spirituality and intense love were the ones who gifted him with an unstoppable determination and sharp intellect.

The time of his childhood was not marked with the fun pursuits of the leisure era, but by the gruelling discipline of the an upcoming kingship. Alexander's life was filled with instruction in archery, riding as well as combat, duties in which he performed admirably with incredible natural talent. In the evenings, he was enthralled by the stories of heroic feats and prophecies of the divine, told by his mother who was adamant about the divine plan for her son.

At a young age Alexander's curiosity was never-ending. Alexander would frequently delve into the pages in his father's library looking for wisdom within the encyclopedias of literature and the complex poems from Homeric epics. But it was beneath the direction of Aristotle the famous philosopher of Athens the Alexander's intellectual development truly began to take shape.

When he was thirteen years, Alexander was sent away to Mieza for a study with Aristotle's keen gaze. The tranquil environment of Mieza and its lush greenery as well as clean flowing rivers, was the ideal setting for their philosophical debates. The teachings of Aristotle are a mixture of philosophy, science art, and politics. He cultivated Alexander's curiosity, as he honed his analytical skills.

"Knowledge," Aristotle would often tell his student, "is the light that dispels the darkness of ignorance." The prince of the future did not hesitate to take these words into consideration. He was immersed in diverse subjects, that ranged from metaphysics to medicine from religion to rhetoric.

Alexander's training was not limited to the pursuit of intellectual knowledge. Aristotle was adamant about the significance of character development as well as ethical behavior. His teachings regarding justice, virtue and courage formed Alexander's moral code and affected the decisions he made throughout his lifetime.

The beginning of a person's greatness doesn't occur by one single occasion but rather an gradual rise illuminated with the soft light of wisdom and a steely determination. When Alexander increased in intelligence and determination under Aristotle's direction and guidance, he started to display those characteristics later to be the hallmarks of his success in the form of strategic brilliance, courageous determination, and an insatiable desire to learn.

At this point in his existence, Alexander was not just getting ready for his kingship, Alexander was planning to change the history books. It was more than the result of ambitions for himself, but one that was going to alter the course of history for all civilizations. The dawn was beginning to break and bringing the rising of one of the world's most powerful individuals the great Alexander the Great.

## Chapter 8: The Ascend to Power

The world was silent on the night of that tragic event when announcement of the assassination by Philip II became a blaze of fire and cast a long, black shadow over the entire kingdom. Within the royal palace, Alexander, his heart was pounding, was able to feel the weight of his father's crown fall upon his head. The weight was not derived from the gold circlet in itself, but because of the huge and unexpected burden that was now on the shoulders of his. It was like fate was guiding him down this arduous path with hardly any warning.

Alexander wasn't born to rule. He was a son second in line who was destined to lead a life under the protection of his brother. But destiny had other plans and it is not uncommon for it to do so. A tragic death of his brother years ago, and then his father's murder had thrown him into a realm which he'd never dreamed of or planned for.

The first few days of his reign were filled with turmoil and uncertain times. The court was split with its loyalty split. A lot of people viewed Alexander's ascendance with suspicion and questioned his legitimacy to govern. The young and unexperienced Alexander meant that he was a prime to target for those seeking to take advantage of the throne's position for personal gain. However, Alexander did not allow himself to be influenced by others.

The first thing he did was rise before dawn each day, and plunged into the world of governance and politics. He was learning how to adapt, change, and becoming. He sought out advice from experienced counsellors and read through old treaties until his eyes began to hurt. He took in the opinions of his people who were concerned about their problems, and made them his personal. Alexander could have been forced into the throne but Alexander refused to be used as a puppet.

"I did not seek this power," the man once admitted to his close adviser, "but now that it is mine, I will wield it for the good of our people."

He skillfully navigated the murky water of intrigue in the palace, overpowering those who wanted to take him under their control. He repelled his opponents not by threats, but through gestures that showed his strength and wisdom. He forged friendships with powerful lords to ensure their loyalty. He reformed law that was unjust, and enacted reforms that helped those in need.

The time passed and the murmurs of doubt became less hushed and replaced with whispers of praise. The court, once divided, began to unite behind their new King. Alexander did not only survive his ascension, he'd been strengthened, his power was unquestioned.

As he consolidated his strength, Alexander had shown a strength that was a testament to his age. He displayed an extraordinary combination of diplomacy and tenacity that won him the respect of the people he served. He was honest and fair and compassionate, yet shrewd. Every decision he took or law he enacted proved his undying devotion to justice and the welfare of his citizens.

In the chaos and confusion in his ascendance to the top, Alexander proved himself as a man who was capable of achieving his title. It did not come without trials and struggles, yet during all of it, Alexander remained unwavering.

Alexander's story was a testimony to his character and strength - his sudden ascendance to power that was wrought with challenges at first and ultimately leading to the reign of a wise and fair rule. The journey of Alexander was an example of optimism in an era that was characterized by turmoil and uncertainty. It was a lesson that the power of a person lies not in bloodline or birthright instead, in one's capacity to earn respect and loyalty through their actions and acts.

Alexander's rise to power was much more than an important moment in his career It was also a symbol of the determination of a country and its citizens. The chapter highlighted the undisputed fact that in even the worst of situations, there is the possibility for the greatest of things.

## Chapter 9: Unifying Greece

The golden sunrise dipped over the cities of Greece the other day, its golden rays announcing the dawn of a new era. In the midst of the transformation was Alexander whose dream of an unification of Greece will alter the direction of history.

As he gazed out at his city Pella The heart of Alexander was full of a desire and not just to his home, but the entire country of Greece. Alexander yeAlexander to be a united country, an entity capable of defending itself against any challenge. The city-states that were scattered all with their distinct goals and alliances, did not have the power that unity can provide.

Alexander's contribution to his role in the unificationAlexander different states played a crucial role. Alexander acted as a beacon of ambition and optimism and gathered city states in his cause with an energy that was powerful as it was inspirational. "Together, we are stronger," said he with his words echoing throughout the rooms of the Amphictyonic Council. His fiery speech and diplomacy gradually impressed even the city states that were most resolute.

Alexandertion from The Hellenic League marked the culmination of Alexander's tireless efforts. It wasn't an easy job that required a careful combination of negotiations, persuasiveness and sometimes, even the use of force. However, Alexander navigated this intricate ballet with skill and aplomb. The vision he had was all Greece that was united by a common banner.

The Hellenic League stood as a testament to Alexander's dedicatAlexandercreation shifted the political landscape, transforming Greece from a collection of individual city-states into a unified entitAlexandernity brought strength, and with strength came unprecedented prosperity and security.

In the midst of whispers and murmurs within the group of Alexanderrs There was a common agreement: Alexander had achieved what was believed to be impossible by many. "The era of division is over," Alexander declared and his eyes sparkled in determination. "Now begins the age of unity."

However, Alexander's vision went beyond the mere unification of politics. Alexander dreamed of an Greece uAlexanderculture and a spirit. He insisted on exchanges between cities and states encouraging shared experiences as well as an understanding of each other. His love for unification ignited the cultural revolution that spanned barriers and touched the hearts of his citizens.

AlejaAlexanderurney didn't come without a setback. Some people resisted his idea, sticking to their old ties and rivalries. But, by utilizing diplomatic sagacity with passionate speeches as well as the sheer determination of his character He was able to win these people in the family. Each challenge just strengthened his determination.

Alexander of Alexander's uniting of Greece is an example of his unwavering determination and his visionary leadership. This is a powerful an example of unity being the most powerful and that the power of a united idea can overcome even the most ferocious divisions.

Alexanderher Day within the unified Greece, Alexander stood tall in the midst of the cities he created. It was a dream that had been made real, but Alexander was aware that this was just the beginning. In the long run, as the challenges that needed to be overcome, and the horizons of possibilities to be conquered, Alexander would stand at the helm, leading his followers towards a more promising the future.

## Chapter 10: The Persian Wars

In the middle in the fifth century BC in the 5th century BC, war that was epic in scope was developing. The scene was set for two of the strongest civilisations in the world of ancient times: Persia, an empire famous for its massive forces and expansive territories as well as a group of cities-states that occupied a tiny piece of land that jutted into the Mediterranean in Greece. It was a simmering conflict that would eventually become what we call The Persian Wars.

The basis of the war was in the imperialistic goals of Persia. Darius the Great Darius the Great, the Persian King was determined to increase the size of his realm, casting his eyes with lust towards city-states in independent cities of Greece. The city-states, however, did not want to fall into his hands without fighting. The catalyst that ignited this conflict came from Ionian Revolt in 499 BC. Ionian Revolt in 499 BC in 499 BC, when Greek cities of Asia Minor, under Persian rule, rebelled against the Persian rulers.

Detailed Battles, Strategies, and Outcomes

The very first major battle is referred to by the name of Battle of Marathon in 490 BC. In spite of being outnumbered by a large margin, the Greeks were steadfast in their stand. They fought back. Athenian general Miltiades employed a novel approach: he reduced the middle of his line, while enforcing the wings. The result was an encircling pincer that eventually surrounded and defeated the Persian troops. The Greek victory in Marathon proved to be a turning point during the conflict.

In the year 480 BC in which the Persians in the reign of King Xerxes began a major attack against Greece. The invasion resulted in two important battles - Thermopylae as well as Salamis. In Thermopylae the small group comprised of Greeks under the leadership of the king Leonidas of Sparta was able to hold off the Persian army in a tiny mountain pass. Though they were ultimately defeated, their strong fighting became a symbol for Greek bravery and determination.

In the meantime, on the sea The Greeks ready to take on the Persian fleet at sea in the Straits of Salamis. Themistocles the Athenian commanding officer, enticed the Persian vessels into water's narrows where their numbers did not matter much. In an intense close-quarters war The agile Greek ships prevailed.

Alexander's leadership Qualities in the Wars

But it is Alexander The Great's leadership throughout his subsequent battles against Persia which truly caught the world's focus. His charisma, as well as his strategic brilliance was evident on the battlefield.

In 334 BC in 334 BC, during the Battle of Granicus, Alexander took his troops through a river, and then up an incline, right into Persian troops. The daring action took the Persians to the ground and earned his first victory over Persia.

His leadership skills were also evident in his participation in the Battle of Gaugamela in 331 BC. Invincible, yet unflinching, Alexander employed an unconventional strategy that capitalized on the weakness of his opponents and he faked a retreat, thereby securing the Persians prior to launching an utterly brutal offensive.

In all of these wars Alexander's determination never waned. His strategic thinking and his unwavering spirit was an example for his soldiers. He led from first line, and was a part of the struggles and trials of his soldiers His actions were much more than any motivational talk could.

Alexander's most famous quote is a perfect description of his leadership style: "I am not afraid of an army of lions led by a sheep; I am afraid of an army of sheep led by a lion."

The battles of the past did not just shape the destiny of Greece and Persia but they also left a lasting impression on the course of world history. They showed how leadership tactics, and courage can overcome all challenges. They painted a vivid image filled with heroic courage, brilliant strategic thinking and perseverance that continue to be awe-inspiring for historians and fans until the present.

## Chapter 11: The Conqueror of Worlds

Even before the sun reached the sky, Alexander was on his horses, his silhouette appearing faint in the bright shades of the dawn. A vast, unexplored expanse of landscapes stretched before him, an inviting mysterious landscape that sounded like the thrill of. It was the only frontier in the globe, an unexplored frontier, which was not touched by the stomping of his troops.

The air shook with the excitement of the unknown the future, and the tension was broken by the thumping of hooves pounding hard-earthed trails. Alexander was not a tourist. Alexander was a conqueror and looked at these unspoiled terrains using a ruler's. The sharpness of his gaze precise, looked out for paths that no existed and towns that were only populated by trees.

However, his vision went beyond territorial annexes. Alexander sought to integrate with a wholesome blend of the customs and traditions during his reign. Every conquered country contained a distinct tapestry of culture and way of living, and Alexander was determined to keep the fibers instead of tearing the fabric.

The way he handled managing was hands-on and a testimony to his unwavering determination. He walked in the crowded markets of cities that had been conquered and his presence was a soothing relief to the angst of those living there. His voice was heard in cities' squares, making decrees promising respect for local customs as well as fair administration.

"Remember," he would affirm, his voice firm yet soft "you are not my subjects, but my people."

The words he spoke of were not empty words. Instead of impositions of his cultural beliefs on conquered territories, Alexander encouraged cultural exchanges. Alexander created a space in which Greek scholars engaged in lively conversations in a heated debate with Persian philosophers beneath

Babylonian skies. Alexander's empire went beyond an area of territory; it was a melting-pot of different civilizations and a testimony to humanity's diversities.

The consequences of these exchanges were significant and forever altered the history of our time. Greek thought filtered through to eastern theories of thought, and Asian artistic styles began to impact Greek aesthetics. The synthesis of cultures was Alexander's legacy and an evidence of his belief that victory was not a matter of dominance, but rather about harmony and harmony.

Through his entire journey, Alexander showed an unflinching determination that inspired the people in his path. In the face of overwhelming odds He did not give up and pushed forward. His spirit of determination served as a lighthouse that illuminated the way for his soldiers even during the most difficult of circumstances.

Alexander wasn't only a conqueror, he was also a bridge that connected different worlds.

His tale is one of strength and ambition, however it is also one of understanding and respect. It is a way to remind us that, even when you're fighting for supremacy there's room for empathy and unity.

The book closes with Alexander is standing on the edge of the world known to us and the wind pulls at the hood of his robe, his gaze focused on the horizon. The sun sets low creating long shadows that highlight the grit that is etched into the face of Alexander. While he travels through unknown territories, he brings alongside him not only the burden of his armor but also the hopes and aspirations of a global community.

So, the story of Alexander the Great, conqueror of all worlds continues to unfold, a epic story which unfolds in the context of the human story we share. From the integrating and management of the conquered territories to major culture exchanges, Alexander's life is an example of his incredible vision and unstoppable determination.

## Chapter 12: The Price of Power

As the sun set over the immense Macedonian Empire as the shadow of Alexander left long shadows on the empire of his rule. An emperor who had once fostered peace and feared against his foes had turned into a shadow of doubt in his own ranks. The change in his approach to leadership, his increasing doubt, and the internal conflict in his own circle could all be signs of an individual who was struggling to pay the cost of his power.

Alexander was once celebrated by his charisma and ability, is now seen as a dictator. His actions, previously lauded because of their boldness and boldness, now were received with a smattering of disapproval. The once dazzling young king had transformed into the sexy king who's gaze was frequently filled with a spooky combination of fear and ambition.

Within the midst of Babylon in the city the place where his throne had gathered conspiracy theories and rumors were frequent. The trusted advisers were viewed by suspicion, while long-time friends were able to elude their own attention. In dimly-lit rooms, voices of suspicion echoed in the dark. A circle once acted in a sign of unity was slowly breaking apart with the pressure of suspicion and power.

In this tension-filled situation, Alexander's relations with his generals continued to be an intricate web of trust, fear and reverence. People who resembled Parmenion and Antigonus who were the foundations of his military strategies and adamantly faithful to the King and their trust unshaken in the midst of the rumours swirling around. Yet, under their unwavering devotion was a stoic understanding that their position was in danger and subject to the will of a man's trust became increasingly hard to keep.

His soldiers knew that Alexander was a mystery to his soldiers an individual to be revered and befeared. Alexander was the one who commanded and led them in fight after battle, with his determination never waning. His speeches, both powerful and inspirational in their power, sparked a deep sense of patriotism inside the troops. But there was a sense of tension. There was a sense that their leader is slowly falling prey to the enticing lure of total power.

Alexander's subjects watched their King from afar, in a state of wonder and fear. Alexander's victories brought fortune and wealth, however the increasingly autocratic regime sparked anxiety. The people watched as their King was transformed from a symbol of hope to an unpredictability power, causing them to contemplate the cost of expanding their empire.

When Alexander traversed the perilous waters of the leadership game, he was continually being reminded that power comes with the cost of a price, a price that was paid through trust, loyalty and tranquility. Every decision he took, every alliance that he made and every fight he engaged in had the weight of the price.

The life of Alexander provides a stark reminding us that power isn't only about dominance or control. It's about balancing between ambition and control as well as suspicion and trust as well as love and fear. Indeed, it is an extremely heavy headdress to wear. It is true that, as Alexander was to discover that the real challenge is not in attaining power, but in utilizing it effectively. His legacy will echo throughout history, the testimony of the man who was able to believe in his dreams, yet he carried the weight of his dreams.

## Chapter 13: Personal Life of a Legend

ALexander's private life was just the same rich and diverse as the huge areas he ruled. His love interests, friends as well as his hobbies portrayed a vivid picture of a man who had more than the average person, however, he was a deeply human.

There was a tight-knit group of acquaintances, derived from as well as the Macedonian elite and the many culture he met during his expeditions. Of them Hephaestion stood out. He was far more than just the friend of a few, but Alexander's closest confidant, close friend, and maybe the only one who could appreciate the extent of his ambitions. The bond they shared, throughout their youth, was defined with mutual respect and unshakeable dedication. When they were on the field they were an imposing powerhouse to reckon with. In the offing they had shared their hopes as well as fears and hopes under the starry skies of far-flung outposts in an empire that was growing ever larger.

His relationships with women were varied and intense. From Roxana an gorgeous Bactrian princess who won his heart by her stunning elegance and sharp mind and Barsine who was the Persian noblewoman who captivated the prince with her sharp wit and insight into his adversaries' home country. Every relationship provided him with an insight into the different diverse cultures that he sought to unify with his authorities.

Alexander's interests were as vast as his vast empire. Alexander had a thirst for knowledge that could not be quenched. It was whether he studied under Aristotle when he was a kid or researching Egyptian divine beings deep in the middle of deserts, Alexander was a student of knowledge, with the same enthusiasm he displayed when he was on the field.

His personality was an exercise of contradictions. He led with iron but listened to his soldiers without a solitary ear. He was ruthless towards the enemy, yet he displayed a tremendous kindness to those who resigned. He longed for immortality however he longed for the basic delights of his returning home.

His values, heavily inspired by his mentor Aristotle as well as his personal experiences focused on the unity of humanity. He imagined an empire in which various cultures and customs were incorporated to form one unified entire.

In Alexander's lifetime were the stories of an unorthodox leader. For instance, the time Alexander quenched his people's thirst, pouring their part of the water over the earth that was dry, saying, "There is no difference in our thirst." And when he slammed those who doubted Bucephalus value by controlling the wild stallion by himself, not just showing his courage but also comprehension of the beast.

The story of Alexander's private life takes you through the heart of a man who's name came to be synonymous with conquer and strength. But, underneath that image of the mighty warrior-king was a brilliant student, a faithful partner, an ardent lover and a visionary who envisioned the world as a united one under a single umbrella.

In this section we've explored some of the less-known facets of Alexander's past, uncovering aspects of his personality that tend to be overlooked in the light of his military accomplishments. The closer examination of his private life provides us with a the chance to take in the legend of Alexander not only as a legendary combatant, but also as an individual who was shaped by his friends as well as his passions, love as well as his beliefs and hopes.

## Chapter 14: "The Downfall"

In the closing chapter of Alexander's story The invincible aura which used to surround him, became dim. Alexander, the great conqueror who's name was echoed throughout the history books, was now facing battles that signaled the onset of his decline.

His health was once strong, but it began declining. Alexander the warrior, who had stood up to defeat on countless battlefields began to succumb to an unfit body that had not could perform as well as it was able to. The strength of his body diminished and his eyes were the same young vigor and energy that was his signature. The once wild animal was slowly becoming the shadow of the man he once was.

An unidentified ailment seized his body, creating a portrait of a man who was frail in sharp contrast to the ferocious soldier he was once. The doctors across the kingdom were baffled with their treatment options ineffective against the nefarious illness that plagued his body. The powerful Alexander was a conqueror of huge lands, was engaged in a battle against his body.

So, his last battles weren't against formidable foes in battle, but rather against unidentified enemies. The battles he fought had no weapon, and nor commanded any troops. He fought on his own and within the limits of his frail body.

"The gods too are mortal," the aforementioned man said to his close friend Hephaestion at some point and his voice carried the burden of acceptance, his eyes shining with an ocean of resigned resignation. His words were a weighty presence across the room, an eloquent warning of the inevitable nature of his downfall.

Alexander's loss was not just physical. Alexander's relationship with his colleagues has always been one of respect, mutual friendship and respect. As his health deteriorated as did his relationships. The people who committed their unwavering loyalty to him started to doubt their loyalty. The rumblings of protest grew more ferocious as they echoed through the palace's halls.

One of the incidents was when an old soldier reacted against him publicly. "You are not the man we once followed," the soldier claimed and his voice was heard throughout the courtroom. Alexander's reaction was silent. He absorbed the criticism in a calm manner and a complete contrast from the flamboyant retort that one would have expected from Alexander from the past.

The causes of Alexander's demise remain a mystery. confusion and speculative speculation. There are those who believe that he passed away from the illness, while some claim the poisoning was caused by. There were even rumors of a plot within his circle.

A hot day in June of 323 B.C., Alexander breathed his final breath. Alexander's death as a conqueror caused shock waves throughout the empire. The world remained silent, as if grieving over the loss of a giant.

His passing marked the close of an era, one that was marked by triumphs as well as conquests, and an unstoppable determination to achieve greatness. Once a formidable conqueror, he fell, leaving behind his legacy which spanned generations. Thus ended the tale of Alexander and his army - but not with a triumphant combat cry, but instead by whispering of his death.

Even in his death Alexander was a mystery and a person as complicated as charismatic. His demise is a stark warning that even the most powerful people in the world aren't immune to the whims of life. The story of his life is an ode to the human spirit's resilience and determination This is a story that is still inspiring admiration and amazement even to this day.

## Chapter 15: The Legacy

In the aftermath of Alexander's demise prematurely at the age of 323 BC in 323 BC, a quiet fell over Babylon. The entire empire was headless in the midst of a gigantic beast stumbling through the chaos. Alexander was not a designated successor or clear sequence of succession established. His abrupt departure created an open space that led to an intense power struggle between his commanders, a battle which would determine the future of the Empire he built.

Although Alexander tried to unite the vast territory under one name, his empire broke up into pieces following his death. The generals he appointed, known as Diadochi who are also known as Diadochi and fought one against the other in a battle for dominance. The wars between the Diadochi that raged for years, culminated in the split of Alexander's empire into three kingdoms principally - Ptolemaic Egypt, Seleucid Mesopotamia and Persia and Antigonid Macedonia. The three kingdoms, in spite of their differences, bore the imprints of Alexander's rule and his vision.

Influence of Alexander penetrated into the foundations of these kingdoms. His system of government as well as his notions of urban planning, as well as his beliefs in acceptance and unity profoundly shaped the societies. These rulers took on the robes of Hellenistic tradition and spread it across their territories. Greek was the first lingua franca to be adopted as well as the amalgamation of the local culture with Greek methods created an unique mix of civilization.

The impact of Alexander's reign extended far beyond his immediate succeeding generations. Alexander's legacy did not limit itself to the boundaries of his former empire, but spread out to reach remote regions around the globe. From Rome through India the rulers sought to replicate Alexander's tactics in war as well as his diplomatic savvy. Alexander's name came to be synonymous with the invincibility of his character, and his life became as a benchmark against that rulers would measure their achievements.

Roman generals adored Alexander as a perfect general, and scrutinized his victories to gain insights. Julius Caesar is said to be crying before the statue of Alexander who was awed by the fact that, while Alexander was a world-class warrior when he was thirty years old, he was a tad mediocre. Napoleon Bonaparte too confessed to having a copy of Alexander's adventures with him throughout his battles.

As influential as he was, Alexander's position in history is the subject that has been the subject of discussion. Certain historians depict Alexander as a dreamer who dreamed of an unifying world. On the other hand, other people see Alexander as a brutal warrior with an endless thirst to be a leader. His determination, his military talents as well as his charismatic leadership style are widely recognized, however there are a variety of opinions on whether to call his character as a hero or criminal.

Contemporary perceptions of Alexander continue to be as varied as the ones from the past. Alexander is still an object of interest and research, with his narrative being adapted into many films and novels. In some circles his name is revered for his role as an advocate of multicultural fusion and diversity, however, in other circles he's criticised as an oppressor his conquests resulted in immense pain and loss.

Whatever the many theories about his character and his legacy, there's any doubt about the significance of Alexander's influence on the history of. His actions and life leave a lasting impression on the Sands of time and shaped the trajectory of civilisations even after the star was been set. The tale of Alexander does not just consist of a ruler or conqueror, but of an idea. It is an idea that's lived through the ages, inspiring generations of people and forever changing the course of our world.

## Chapter 16: Alexander and Us

Alexander The Great was a person of determination and vision, is an inspiration for leadership, who's story spans generations, influencing the society which we are living today. Lexander's lessons remain within our hearts, revealing the blueprint for leaders of the future and those who dream. In this chapter, we'll travel through time and look at the important lessons that he had to leave in his wake, and the effect he has had on the present society and then, a reflection on his extraordinary life.

Alexander was more than the conqueror, Alexander was also a man with determination and perseverance. In the twilight years of twenty-one, he was elevated to the throne following the assassination of his father the King Philip II of Macedon. The period could have been one of time when the country was in a state of crisis for Macedonia and its people, however Alexander was able to hold the throne by securing them with his firm hand. Alexander, a young king brimming by a burning need to increase his kingdom, commenced an undertaking that could alter the direction of the history.

One of his best-known experiences was at Gordium the place where he had to contend with an intricate knot which nobody had been able to unravel. Instead of giving in to anger or escaping the task, Alexander drew his sword and cut it open with a powerful strike. The episode teaches an important idea that there are many solutions to a problem and sometimes it takes the use of unconventional methods.

Alexander's influence in our current society is significant. Alexander's vision of integrating culture led to the birth of Hellenistic culture, a mix with Greek and Eastern traditions - and has shaped our society with subtle ways. This can be observed in a myriad of areas, such as architecture, art, or the study of philosophy. The man who taught us the meaning of unity and diversity which is a concept that has relevance more than ever in a increasingly globalized world.

When dealing with his soldiers, Alexander demonstrated remarkable empathy and emotional ability. Alexander often dined alongside his troops, heard their complaints, and even stood with them on battle - which is a striking contrast to managers who choose to manage from their castles. His actions are a reminder that effective leadership requires being aware of and responding to the needs and needs of those who we are responsible for.

Alexander's personal life wasn't without imperfections or contention. Alexander's temper was notorious and his ambition frequently resulted in ruthless choices. These aspects, however, are not a detriment to the value of his accomplishments; rather they elevate him to a higher level. The truth is that even the greatest of people do not exempt themselves from failings.

When we look back at Alexander's journey We can see a person who was driven by a constant thirst to learn and explore. Alexander sought out wisdom from philosophers, participated in discussions of scholarly merit as well as a constant fascination with the surroundings. His experiences serve to remind us that education is a continuous process.

Alexander's journey is testament to the strength of mankind. His life's story is a reminder that through determination, courage and creative thinking we are able to overcome challenges and make our way to the next level. When we live our daily lives within this complicated world, let's be reminded of Alexander Not just as a conqueror, but also as a visionary who dare to imagine and turned these dreams into reality.

## Chapter 17: Alexander

Alexander the Great, born in the year 356 BCE at Pella, Macedonia, was one of the world's most important people. He was elevated to the throne when he was just 20 years old after the assassination and murder of his father the King Philip II of Macedon . Since his earliest years, Alexander displayed exceptional military skills, as well as strategic thinking and an appetite for victory.

Under the leadership of Alexander under Alexander, under Alexander's leadership, the Macedonian Empire expanded its borders by launching a string of impressive combats. One of his first victory was to defeat the Persian Empire - a massive and powerful empire that been threatening the Greek cities for a long time. In 334 BCE He conquered the Hellespont by deploying the help of a force of 35,000 troops, and began an unstoppable battle for the conqueror.

Alexander's wartime campaigns led the army across Asia Minor, Egypt, and Persia in which

Alexander won many battles and took control of vast areas. Alexander employed innovative strategies including the fast and decisive cavalry attacks of his famed Companion Cavalry, to secure victory against forces that were numerically superior.

In the year 331 BCE, Alexander achieved a significant victory during the Battle of Gaugamela which saw him defeat the Persian ruler Darius III and solidifying his authority of his empire. Persian Empire. After the demise of the Persian Empire, Alexander continued his expansion to the east, venturing to Central Asia, India, as well as beyond. The empire spanned across Greece through Egypt and stretched to the Indus River.

Alexander's victories in war did not just result from the battle. Alexander also sought to promote Greek concepts and culture that is why he was referred to as Hellenism. This was accomplished through the construction in Greek cities as well as the blending of the local culture, as well as the integration between Greek and Eastern practices. In the end, his work became the catalyst to exchange knowledge and concepts between Greek and Eastern civilisations.

Despite his impressive military skills his ambitious campaigning resulted in a loss for the army he commanded and also him. Alexander's Macedonian troops endured long, gruelling treks through harsh terrain and fought numerous battles that resulted in a lot of casualties. In 323 BCE following many years of constant warfare, Alexander succumbed to a mysterious disease at Babylon in the year 32.

The passing of Alexander the Great was the beginning of an era, and it resulted in a period of unstable times as his empire split into smaller states ruled by the generals he appointed, also known as Diadochi. However, his legacy remained. Alexander's victories had an indelible mark upon the areas he conquered by spreading Greek tradition, language and concepts across an enormous region and influencing the course of human history.

Through time, Alexander the Great has been hailed as a genius in the field of warfare and a leader of vision as a symbol of determination and ambition. Alexander's legacy has inspired and continues to enthrall generations to come, and the impact he had over the world of antiquity can't be understated.

Alexander's childhood played an important influence on his personality and aspirations. He was educated thoroughly by the renowned philosopher Aristotle and his followers, who instilled in his son a passion for studying philosophical concepts, philosophy, as well as the arts. The education he received had a significant influence on Alexander who sparked his academic fascination and appreciation of Greek cultural and intellectual knowledge.

Training for the Troop

One of the most distinctive characteristics of Alexander was his ability to incite and guide his soldiers. He frequently fought with his troops, earning their trust and respect. His leadership charisma and his personal strength were a motivation behind his soldiers' indefatigable determination and readiness to fight alongside him in most difficult fights.

Alexander's strategies for military were marked by a high degree of flexibility, scalability as well as an in-depth knowledge of his adversaries and weaknesses. Alexander utilized a mixture of fast cavalry attacks with phalanx formations, methods of siege warfare to take on the most formidable adversaries. The strategic genius of his was demonstrated during the world-renowned Siege of Tyre, where He constructed a causeway that would connect the mainland with the island town, which demonstrated his innovative and determined thinking.

Apart from his victories in the battlefield, Alexander had a vision of unification and a desire to bring different cultures together. He exhorted his soldiers to get married Persian females, urged the acceptance of Persian traditions, and adopted some elements of Persian traditional practices including proskynesis. which is a type of respect, and the obeisance. However, this caused tensions with his Macedonian colleagues, who saw this as an aversion to their Greek tradition.

In the course of his campaign, Alexander founded several cities and named them for his own, with the most renowned of which was Alexandria within Egypt. The cities were places of Greek cultural, trade and administration, encouraging exchange of ideas and understanding between civilizations. They were also important centers of research and learning including academies, libraries, and other institutions that attracted scientists, philosophers, as well as scholars from different regions.

In spite of his victories in war, Alexander faced numerous challenges and defeats. The army was swarmed by formidable adversaries and was a victim of mutinies within his army, and also had to put down rebellions within areas he had conquered. The arduous expedition to India challenged the capabilities of his army, and led to a decline in morale. This led to his soldiers' disinclination to travel towards the east.

Following Alexander's death, the empire was divided and his generals battled to take control. The Hellenistic period following was marked by a power struggle and the creation of various successor states that competed to be the most powerful. The influence of culture and the legacy of Alexander's victories was able to influence the areas throughout the centuries that followed.

Alexander The Great's effect in the history of mankind cannot be understated. The military victories of his time changed the geography of the early world, and spread Greek concepts and culture that extended beyond the borders of the empire he ruled. His reputation as a masterful army strategist, leader with vision and bridge-builder of culture is still capturing the attention of millions around the world and make his name one of the greatest and most beloved people.

The most notable thing about Alexander's reign is his dedication in promoting and advancing the literature, arts as well as philosophical thought. Alexander was surrounded by poets, scholars and intellectuals, setting up an intellectually stimulating atmosphere in the court of his. Famous individuals like Callisthenes the nephew of Aristotle, and philosopher Anaxarchus were with the king on his journeys encouraging intellectual debates and exchange of ideas.

Battle against Persian Empire

Alexander's relationship to his relationship with Persian Empire and the Persian people is fascinating. When he battled against Persian troops, he showed respect for the Persian culture. He practiced the Persian practices, got married to an Persian noblewoman called Roxana and promoted intermarrying between his troops as well as Persian women. The goal of this policy was to promote an integration of cultures and aid the building in his empire.

In the course of his battles, Alexander encountered various legendary people, including the Indian King Porus which he famously defeated at his famous Battle of Hydaspes. Porus's strength and courage amazed Alexander enough that Alexander restored Porus as the local ruler. He even made him one of his Satraps (governors).

A significant moment that Alexander was involved in was his trip to his visit to the Oracle of Amun in Siwa Oasis in Egypt. Looking for divine confirmation that he was truly his father Alexander was able to receive confirmation that he indeed was Zeus-Ammon's son. The affirmation further reinforced the faith of his own and added to the divine aura which surrounded his image in the eyes of his soldiers and subordinates.

While he is most well-known for his victories in the military, Alexander also pursued other exciting tasks. Alexander started the great endeavor of cataloguing the knowledge by requesting an enormous collection dubbed The Library of Alexandria. This library was intended to accumulate and protect the world's information with a wealth of scrolls attracting scholars from every corner of the world.

In tragic circumstances, Alexander's existence was ended when he was a young man and his empire was left in turmoil and confusion. After his demise the body of his remains was buried in a golden sarcophagus before being transferred to Alexandria and has become a symbol of respect. The cause of the death of his father is a matter of discussion and theories range between malaria and poison.

Alexander's life and his achievements are the inspiration for countless literary works, artwork and cinema throughout through the ages. His tale continues to stir the imagination and remains a representation of exceptional determination, military genius and the exchange of culture. His reputation as one of the greatest powerful and feared figures can be seen in his profound influence upon the world.

Alexander's wars did not stop at on the ground; there was also a large naval force. Alexander commissioned the building of the world's largest fleet of ships, which had a major role to play in maintaining control of key areas of the coast and in facilitating his victories. The victories he won in naval conflicts like The Battle of Issus and the Battle of Issus and the Battle of Tyre showcased his capabilities as a commander and his ability to be a leader in naval and land warfare.

In the course of his rule , Alexander encountered numerous challenges and encountered significant resistance. One of the most memorable was the intense resistance against him from the Tyre city. Tyre. The battle for Tyre ran for seven months which demonstrated the strength and determination of both Alexander's troops and Tyrians. In the end, Alexander's troops won, which led to the destruction and capture of Tyre's city.

One of the main aspects of Alexander's empire is the integration between Greek and Eastern culture. This amalgamation of civilizations and cultures, referred to as Hellenistic culture, led to the spreading of Greek languages, art as well as philosophy and architecture throughout the areas which he defeated. The process also led to the development of Greek-style cities that served as hubs of commerce, administration and even culture, encouraging an atmosphere of harmony and the exchange of culture.

Alexander's influence was not limited to the battlefields he fought. Alexander was a key player in the promotion of Greek literary and philosophical thought, assuring the survival and diffusion of the works of famous poets and philosophers. His ties with philosopher

Callisthenes was the reason for the translating of Persian texts in Greek which further enhanced the cultural culture and his empire.

Despite his victories in battle, Alexander faced internal opposition from his generals and soldiers tired of his constant battles. In the Battle of the Hyphasis River in India the troops of Alexander were unable to move further east and forced him to renounce his plan to expand further. It was a pivotal moment in his victories as his troops' morale sank as the size of his empire strains the loyalty of his troops.

Alexander's legacy has had an enormous influence on the generations to come. In the years following his death the cult of his personality developed, with him considered a godlike character. The descendants of his successors, often referred to as Diadochi Diadochi battled for their control over the vast kingdom, leading to an era of conflict and territorial divides. The Hellenistic kingdoms which were established maintained certain aspects of Greek tradition and exercised influence over the territories they administered.

To conclude, Alexander the Great's life was distinguished by his successes in the field of warfare, a dream of fusion between cultures, as well as a desire for knowledge. The victories of his army changed the course of history and world, making an irresistible impression on history, and leaving an legacy that remains acknowledged and studied even to the present. His remarkable leadership along with his brilliant strategic thinking and his influence in the world of culture confirm his status among the world's notable historical figures.

## Chapter 18: Alexander's leadership

Alexander's leadership spanned beyond his conquers of the military. He instituted administrative reforms that to integrate those he had conquered in his empire. The local authorities were appointed by him to oversee the administration and made sure that rituals and beliefs were observed and maintained the stability of the country and created a feeling of unity between the diverse population.

In his travels, Alexander encountered various natural challenges and natural wonders. One of them was his legendary trek through the dangerous Hindu Kush Mountains. In spite of the extreme conditions and hostile tribes perseverance and shrewdness helped him overcome the obstacles and carry on his journey to conquer.

One of Alexander's greatest heroic acts occurred at his time at the Battle of the Granicus River. In charge of the battle as the leader of his cavalry unit, he took on troops from the enemy, showing immense courage, and bringing his troops to win. The hands-on way of fighting has earned him appreciation and respect from his fellow soldiers.

Alexander's legacy is not limited to the accomplishments of his military and culture. Alexander made important contributions to exploration and science in addition. He solicited the help of famous scholars, including Onesicritus and Nearchus who were with the king on his expeditions and recorded the flora, fauna and the geography of the territories that he fought. Their work provided invaluable information regarding previously undiscovered areas.

Despite his ambitions for military, Alexander showed a deep fascination with philosophy, and sought out the wisdom of renowned philosophers who were influential in his time. He was involved in philosophical debates with philosophers, such as Diogenes and Diogenes the Cynic and was heavily in the direction of Heraclitus. The philosophical discussions he had with these philosophers led to the development of his mind and his view of the world and his leadership.

Alexander's influence was felt in the field of architecture as well as urban design. Cities he established like Alexandria in Egypt as well as Bactra today in Afghanistan was meticulously planned and embellished with elaborate buildings, such as temples, palaces as well as theaters. They became the centers of commerce, culture and education, leaving long-lasting architecture and cultural heritage.

One of the most notable aspects of Alexander's persona was his deep reverence for his father his king, Philip II. Alexander considered himself to be the successor to his father's dreams and believed his obligation to meet the same goals and exceed his father's ambitions. The military campaign he fought was in order to not only expand his empire, but also to take revenge on his father's demise and preserve his place in history.

The character of Alexander the Great has inspired numerous myths and romances through time. Alexander's victories, his charisma as well as his divine aura surrounding his life have captivated the imagination of poets, writers and even artists for many centuries. From the ancient Greek writing to contemporary film and literature His story will continue to be told and celebrated.

To conclude, Alexander the Great's biography is an eloquent testimony of his extraordinary accomplishments as a leader in the military who was a visionary as well as ambassador for culture. The legacy of his time encompasses the military's skill and cultural fusion as well as academic pursuits, and architecture achievements. His battles and life remain an illustration of humanity's determination, perseverance and the quest for excellence.

Alexander's campaigns in the military weren't limited to the territorial and naval victories. Alexander also set out on a long-distance journey to discover the unexplored regions that lie within his Indian subcontinent. The journey led him across treacherous terrains, through rivers, and interacting with diverse civilizations and kingdoms. This was the time that Alexander's soldiers were confronted with some of their greatest obstacles.

One of the most important fights waged by Alexander from India included his Battle of Hydaspes , where the king was defeated by Porus and his troops. Even though he was outnumbered Porus stood up to a ferocious fight, using battle elephants, as well as a more strategic defensive line. Yet, Alexander's tactical savvy along with the discipline and determination of his soldiers ensured victory. Admired by the bravery of Porus, Alexander treated him with respect and permitted him to remain in his realm under his rule.

Alexander's impact on the territories that he conquered wasn't only via the use of force. Alexander also implemented strategies that promoted commerce, trade, as well as cultural exchange. He promoted the expansion of trade routes including the famous Silk Road, connecting the East and West. It allowed for the exchange of products technology, ideas, and concepts among different cultures.

In the course of his travels, Alexander encountered the renowned philosopher and ascetic Diogenes from Sinope. The meeting they had in Corinth was the focus of a myriad of stories. Diogenes is well-known as a skeptic of things of material value, was said to have told Alexander to walk away and not block the sun. This conversation left a mark on Alexander and he admired Diogenes's philosophy and his the non-conformist way of life.

Alongside his victories in the war, Alexander embarked on a task to promote Greek culture and civilisation. He fought for the adoption of the Greek cultural, customs as well as the educational system in the territories that he took on. He set up educational institutions that were modeled upon those of the Lyceum and Academy of Athens which ensured the diffusion of Greek ideas and philosophy.

Alexander's demise triggered an internal struggle for power among his commanders, dubbed "the Wars of the Diadochi. These wars resulted into the splitting of the empire into multiple Hellenistic kingdoms, each one governed by one general. The successor states, like those of the Seleucid Empire, the Ptolemaic Kingdom and the Antigonid Kingdom have continued to be in existence for a number of decades and played a major influence on the development of historical events.

The legacy left by Alexander the Great was influential to the later civilisations. Alexander's achievements as well as strategies for building empires were a blueprint for conquerors to come, such as Julius Caesar and Napoleon Bonaparte. His name has become synonymous with determination and military success which inspired many great leaders across history.

Alexander's story remains a topic of debate and fascination. Archaeologists and historians are still discovering new information regarding his life and battles by studying ancient writings, discoveries from archaeology as well as scientific studies. In spite of the passing of time, Alexander the Great's impact on the course of history is unquestionable which has made him among the top significant people to ever live.

Alexander's military operations

Alexander's wars weren't limited to conquer of land and the creation of empires. The goal was also to propagate Greek ideas and culture by claiming himself to be an educator and benefactor to all of the world. He was determined to unify all the different cultures within his empire into a single Hellenistic culture, while blending Greek as well as local customs.

While on his quests, Alexander encountered and incorporated different religious beliefs within the empire he ruled. Alexander paid respect to gods and respected the spiritual practices of the people he conquered. In Egypt where he was regarded as the pharaoh. He also believed in the Egyptian divinity Amun. In Babylon the city, he was a part of rituals of worship and revered his Babylonian gods.

Alexander's military operations were not only motivated by the expansion and conquest of his empire. He also sought to destabilize the Persian Empire's power and seek revenge for the past invasions against Greece. The campaign was seen by him as legitimate reasons to free the Greek city-states as well as secure their liberation from Persian control.

Although he won numerous times, Alexander faced considerable resistance in certain areas and faced intense resistance. One of the most famous examples was his battle against the mountains of the northwestern region of the Indian subcontinent. There, he had to face a number of formidable enemies, such as the ferocious tribes in the region. The battles he had with Indian King Porus and the infamous Nanda Empire test his ability to lead and for military strength.

Alexander's egocentric nature and desire to be admired by others sometimes caused him to take impulsive actions which led to instances of extreme violence and brutality. An example is the brutal murder of Thebes, his city Thebes who had rebelled against the rule of Alexander. This brutal act of violence sent an explicit message to the other cities and towns that were under his control, demanding the obedience and respect of.

Alexander's life was characterized by complicated relations. He had multiple marriages and took upon Persian wives, and making unions by marriage with noble families of the territories he conquered. His most notable marriage took place to Roxana who was the daughter of an Bactrian nobleman, and with who the couple had a son called Alexander IV. The marriages and alliances were designed to consolidate his power and to create a sense unification among his people.

Apart from the military and political accomplishments, Alexander had a keen fascination with exploration and discovering. Alexander urged his generals and officers to embark on expeditions in search of new territories and to discover natural wonders that were not previously known. His efforts opened new routes for trade, promoted the study of geography, and also contributed to the advancement of the understanding of science in fields like botany and zoology.

Alexander's sudden death at 32 put his empire in the midst of uncertainty, and led to a period of unstable. The cause of his death was an idea that he had been an innocent victim of a plot and that he was the victim of a conspiracy, however historical reports indicate that the cause was an untimely illness, which could be malaria or the typhoid virus. His death marked the conclusion of an era, and created the conditions for the disintegration of the empire into smaller ones.

The image of Alexander the Great remains a magnet for the imagination and arouse fascination. Alexander's life and victories were the focus of numerous literary works as well as art and film that portray the hero as legendary and symbol of excellence. His story is an illustration of the incredible achievements that are possible with determination, determination, and a strategic approach.

Through his campaign, Alexander encountered and engaged in diplomatic relationships with a variety of prominent figures of the time. Alexander had conversations with some of the most famous philosophers like the important Stoic philosopher Zeno of Citium and later the creator of the Stoic school of thinking. The encounters helped him gain a better understanding of different philosophical systems and contributed to his own personal intellectual development.

Alexander's strategies for military were not restricted to confrontation with direct force. The strategist also utilized psychological techniques to conquer his foes. In the case of attack on the island city of Tyre the city of Tyre, he built a causeway connecting the mainland towards the city. He demonstrated the strength of his resolve and ability to conquer seemingly impossible obstacles. The psychological battle weakened the will of Tyrians Tyrians and resulted in the eventual surrender of Tyre.

The reign of Alexander was not only marked by war but he also held the idea of cultural integration. He advocated for the mixing with Greek, Persian, and different local traditions, creating the feeling of unity in his. empire. He encouraged intermarriage between soldiers of his empire as well as women from the local community, which led to the birth of a brand new generation, which embodied the fusion of different cultures.

As a leader Alexander demonstrated his leadership by example and shared the struggles of his men. Alexander was active in fighting which often saw him with his troops, earning his the respect and trust of his soldiers. He was willing to take time to take the time to listen to the complaints, respond to their issues and acknowledge their courage and build a connection between him and his troops.

Alexander's dreams extended to the boundaries of his own world. According to old accounts that he was adamant to go beyond the bounds of earth and explore new territories. According to legend, he wept when his men did not want to continue their march eastward towards the Hyphasis River, as he believed that there were unknown territories to explore and wonders waiting for his arrival.

Through his entire life, Alexander showed a deep love of the arts and the culture. Alexander was awed by the work of Homer and carried copies of the Iliad along on his travels, and aimed to resemble the hero figures in the classic Greek epics. Also, he had a huge support for the arts by requesting famous designers and artists to make works of art in his new cities. He left a long-lasting creative heritage.

In spite of his huge military achievements the Alexander's goal was not only. The focus was on conquest. The vision he had was unifying his two worlds of East as well as the West in a harmonious civilisation by blending the best aspects of each world. He favored the exchange of knowledge, ideas and commerce between various areas, encouraging the development of intellectual and cultural.

In the years following his death, many mythologies and legends about Alexander the

Great arose and affirmed his status as a giant. They helped to make him a hero as well as the development of an epic story of his career and accomplishments. They also played an integral part in establishing his posthumous fame as a renowned ruler as well as a source of inspiration.

In the end, Alexander the Great's biography can be seen as a testimony to the diversity of his personality and influence on the world of ancient times. His strength in battle, culture integration efforts, academic activities, and qualities of leadership are what make him a person of fascination and research. Its legacy will continue to be awe-inspiring for researchers, historians, and admirers and make him one of the most revered figures in the history of humanity.

Alexander's influence grew beyond his cultural and military achievements. Alexander implemented reforms to the administration that focused on improving administration and establish a more efficient bureaucracy in the empire he ruled. He created a system of satraps who served as regional governors. They also implemented standardized coins, weights and measurements, which helped in ensuring growth and stability in the economy while also facilitating trade.

In all his battles, Alexander showed a remarkable capacity to learn and adapt from various culture. Alexander sought out the advice of local advisers, adopted the local traditions. And he incorporated foreign soldiers into his military. His flexible and open approach helped him to earn the respect and trust of a variety of groups, thus ensuring stabilization and management of his huge empire.

Despite his victories in war, Alexander faced challenges and internal discord within his groups. Alexander's policies of integration and intermarrying with people he had conquered was met with opposition from a few members of his Macedonian generals, who perceived his policies as an attack on their position of power. It led to a host of tensions and conspiracies and highlighted the delicate balance that he had to preserve as a ruler.

A visionary leader, Alexander had grand ambitions to spread Greek knowledge and culture. Alexander founded a number of cities, most often called Alexandria throughout his vast empire. They became centres of education, with academic institutions and libraries, which attracted scholars from all over of the globe. Most famous among them is The Library of Alexandria, which contained a huge library of texts from the past and was a key factor in the transmission and conservation of information.

Alexander's wars weren't just about conquering, but also to secure crucial strategic positions as well as trade routes. Alexander understood the value having control over key regions like Egypt that gave the opportunity to access lucrative trade routes as well as sources. The conquests of his empire widened Greek influence, and also opened many new business opportunities for his empire and the future of civilizations.

One of Alexander's longest-lasting legacy is his spread in the Greek language, now known by the name of Koine Greek, which became the main lingua franca in the eastern Mediterranean as well as of the Near East for centuries. The influence of the language created the base to an development of a common cultural and intellectual heritage in the sense that Greek evolved into the official language of business, administration and even education.

Alexander's war campaigns weren't exclusively focused on conquest or dominance. The Alexander campaign also promoted Greek concepts of liberty and democracy and encouraged local communities to adopt these ideals in their management. He also advocated the creation of democratic institutions in certain areas, and encouraged a feeling of belonging and empowerment for the population who live there.

In all his years, Alexander demonstrated a deep admiration of the feats of his hero, Achilles, as depicted in the Homer's Iliad. Alexander sought to imitate Achilles his heroic traits such as courage honour, integrity, and the desire for glory. The admiration for Achilles influenced his strategies for military and personal behavior, forming his image as a king who fought for his people.

The fascination that has remained in Alexander the Great is due to his incredible achievements and the lasting effect of his conquers. Alexander's life story is the ultimate example of determination, leadership and an obsession with excellence. His impact on later civilizations as well as his imposing personality remain awe-inspiring and encourage admiration for his incredible achievements and life.

## Chapter 19: Individual sacrifices

Alexander's battles in the military did not come without sacrifices. Alexander endured physical pain with his troops, shouldering their struggles and showing his strength as the leader. He was a role model with his remarkable physical endurance and stamina, often walking long distances, and participating in battles, despite injuries and ailments.

As a ruler Alexander sought to encourage the unity of his people and encourage a sense of camaraderie among his many subject. He advocated for intermarrying among Greeks as well as non-Greeks. He emphasized the fusion of cultures as well as creating a sense of a shared destiny. The policy of cultural integration was designed to build a unified empire, and lessen tensions between people who were conquered as well as the Greek conquerors.

Alexander's leadership skills and charisma brought him the respect and respect of his troops. He forged strong bonds to his troops, and was able to reward their devotion with generous presents and awards. They exhibited unwavering loyalty and dedication to the cause, regardless the most difficult of circumstances.

In the course of his battles, Alexander encountered various legends and mythologies which shaped the way he saw himself and the path he was on. Alexander believed that he was a descendants of Achilles and proclaimed a divine lineage that traced his roots all the way to mythical heroes like Heracles. The beliefs fuelled his drive and affirmed his belief that he was meant to achieve greatness.

Alexander's wars during the Persian Empire have had a major influence on the culture of the region and social structure. The Hellenistic influence grew rapidly which led to the incorporation of Greek architecture, aesthetics and philosophy into the local customs. The fusion of different culture, also known as Hellenization had an impact that lasted for a long time on the literature, arts as well as the architecture of regions that were taken over.

In spite of his achievements, Alexander faced setbacks and difficulties. His soldiers were afflicted with fatigue and fatigue, which led to insubordination, as well as mutiny. The commander had to use a variety of methods to ensure discipline and maintain the spirits of his troops at a high level. There were logistical issues to manage his huge empire, which included supply shortages and the requirement to navigate various administrative and cultural systems.

Alongside his victories in the war, Alexander had a keen fascination with scholarship and other intellectual activities. Alexander's circle was filled with famous scholars, philosophers, and academics, such as Aristotle and Aristotle, who coached him in his early years. Alexander's love of studies and arts helped bring about a renaissance of the arts within the areas which he fought, resulting in improvements in a variety of fields of study.

Alexander's tragic death at 32 put his empire in an uneasy state and uncertainty. There was no clear successor led to an internal struggle for power among his generals, referred to as Diadochi. In the Wars of the Diadochi led to the division of his empire into several kingdoms. This marked the conclusion of an era of unification of the Hellenistic empire.

The influence from Alexander the Great is still felt throughout the history of. His victories had an enormous impact on the territories which he conquered and shaped their culture, political as well as social terrains throughout the centuries. His strategies for war along with his leadership abilities as well as his cultural perspectives have continued to influence and inspire strategists and leaders to this today.

In the end, Alexander the Great's biography can be seen as a testimony to his remarkable leadership skills as well as his ambition and vision. His military skill, his academic endeavors, and the ability to cross cultures made an impact in the course of history. His status being one of the top significant people in the history of mankind is still evident which makes him a timeless icon of inspiration and greatness.

Alexander's war-related campaigns weren't limited to only conquering land. Alexander was also involved in a large naval mission, including the capturing of key coastal cities, as well as the development military bases. Victories in naval battles across the Aegean Sea and in the Eastern Mediterranean established his authority on vital trade routes through the maritime sector and further widened the reach of his empire.

Alongside his political and military endeavors, Alexander displayed a deep admiration for the sciences and arts. He was a staunch supporter of the works of philosophers, scientists, scholars as well as scientists. He also encouraged the pursuit and conservation of information. He founded the renowned Library of Alexandria in Egypt and it became a world-renowned place of study and also housed an impressive library of scrolls and books that came from different civilizations.

Alexander's interest in exploration extended to the natural world too. Alexander was joined by scientists, historians and naturalists during his expeditions and document the wildlife, flora as well as the geography of the places he explored. These explorations led to more thorough understanding of the globe's diversity and the geography of the same time.

In spite of his victories in the military, Alexander had a diplomatic part and sought to form peace-loving alliances with the kingdoms of his neighbors. Alexander recognized the importance to maintain stability while secure cooperation from the neighboring. powers. Through treaties and diplomatic marriages the king forged friendships that provided mutual benefit and decreased the need for constant war.

In his lifetime, Alexander demonstrated a progressive approach to women. He granted women a degree of autonomy and power that was not found in the ancient world. Alexander respected the opinions of women who were influential, such as his mother Olympias as well as sought advice from powerful women such as Cleopatra, the Egyptian Queen Cleopatra. His gender-neutral approach was instrumental in shaping the role and position of women throughout his empire.

Alexander's influence did not only extend to the countries which he conquered during his time. The Hellenistic period that began following his demise, saw the expansion of Greek civilization, language and customs throughout the east of the Mediterranean, Asia, and further afield. Greek became the language of the elites who were educated and Greek concepts and artistic expression thrived throughout the centuries within the lands of his victories.

Despite his accomplishments and ambitions the reign of Alexander was ineffective. The untimely demise of his empire in danger of internal battles as well as external dangers. His legacy was marked by a string of conflict and struggle for power that eventually led to split and the demise of his empire.

The tale of Alexander the Great remains a fascination for researchers, historians and even fans. His life and his achievements demonstrate the amazing feats that can be achieved with the power of determination, vision and strategically-minded thought. His lasting influence on victories, his culture and intellectual achievements, as well as his unique character make him a enduring person in the history of our world.

In the end, Alexander the Great's biography is a stunning account of a man with a formidable military background and intellectual interests, as well as political vision and cultural abilities shaped the world of ancient times. Alexander's legacy as a conqueror of the world, visionary, and a champion of the sciences and arts is still inspiring generations of people and creates a permanent mark in the history of mankind. historical events.

**Chapter 20: Alexander's desire to drink**

One of the most distinctive features of Alexander's life was his insatiable desire for information. He was a fervent advocate for knowledge and actively sought advice and wisdom from famous philosophers and scholars. With the help of Aristotle He discovered a passion for the arts, philosophy, and sciences, and this was a major influence on his academic pursuits throughout his lifetime.

Alexander's love of the old world and the mythology that inspired him to discover and overcome. He set off on treks to places of legend, like Troy, the city Troy and made a homage to mythological heroes from the ancient past. The connection to mythological stories and the belief in his divine lineage gave a mythological element to his battles.

In all his battles, Alexander faced formidable adversaries and fought in fights that became the subject of legends. Alexander defeated his foes in the Persian Empire, overcame the formidable Darius III at the Battle of Gaugamela. Darius III at the Battle of Gaugamela as well as took on Egypt, India, and huge areas of Asia. The strategies he employed in his military and strategic skill enabled him to defeat the odds to win.

Alongside his accomplishments in the military, Alexander was a visionary city planner as well as architect. Alexander founded a number of cities across the empire. They were all carefully placed in order to facilitate the administration of trade and cultural exchange. Cities like Alexandria in Egypt were flourishing as commercial and cultural centers featuring the merging of Greek as well as local customs.

Alexander's charismatic personality and captivating persona elicited unwavering loyalty admiration from his fans. Alexander had a charismatic aura and could invigorate his troops through his speeches, strength and tenacity. His troops regarded his status as a quasi-mythical character and would be his followers to the end of the globe.

Known for his battles with the military, Alexander also implemented policies that aimed to improve the lives of his people. Alexander instituted administrative reforms as well as abolished taxes that were oppressive and encouraged the introduction of regional customs and language. The way he governed was to maintain the security and stability of his vast empire.

Alexander's influence was far beyond achievements in politics and military. His legacy was a major influence on his legacy throughout the past, and left a long-lasting impression on the areas which he defeated. The Hellenistic period that followed his rule saw the fusion between Greek, Persian, and Egyptian culture, which resulted in an extensive cultural mosaic and the exchange of knowledge which led to advancements in a variety of disciplines.

In the aftermath of the death of Alexander, his empire fell apart between his generals. This led to the development of powerful dynasties. The Hellenistic kingdoms which emerged after Alexander's conquests shaped and shape the Mediterranean as well as the Near Eastern regions for centuries. Greek art, language and even philosophy influenced the successor states.

The fascination that has remained with Alexander the Great is in his capacity to override time and be a lasting emblem of excellence and ambition. Alexander's extraordinary victories, his intelligent pursuits, strategic genius as well as his larger-than-life personality remain awe-inspiring to the minds of all people of existence.

To conclude, Alexander the Great's biography can be a testimony of his incredible successes, intellect, as well as his leadership capabilities. The strength of his spirit, his strength in battle, and a an enlightened mindset helped him become among the top significant individuals in history. The impact of his victories along with his intellectual and cultural contributions and the lasting legacy have made him a timeless icon of excellence and inspiration.

Alexander's wars were marked by several important battles. Alexander employed his innovative strategies and the use of siege engines in order to defeat the fortifications of cities that were heavily fortified, like Tyre as well as Gaza. These sieges showed his strategic power and determination, and also his capacity to modify his tactics according to meet the specific challenges faced by every city.

Through his many conquests Alexander tried to blend and blend the culture of the countries that he defeated. He encouraged the intermarrying of Greeks and non-Greeks by encouraging intercultural exchanges and blending of cultures. The policy of cultural fusion is referred to in the term "syncretism," allowed for the preservation of traditional customs as well as spreading Greek influence.

The most striking features of Alexander's reign was his religious stance. In honoring the gods in the Greek pantheon, he demonstrated a remarkable acceptance of different religious beliefs held by the people he served. He wanted to portray him as liberator, and an unifying power, while respecting the deities of the region and incorporating these into his own spiritual rituals.

Alexander's expeditions to India represented the highest point of his conquers. Alexander's encounters against Indian kingdoms, like Porus, the mighty leader Porus and the powerful ruler Porus, testified to his strength as a soldier and demonstrated the capacity to adapt to new terrains and strategies. Even though he faced challenges, and the unwillingness of his troops the king was able to win victory and extend his power to his own Indian subcontinent.

Under his stewardship, Alexander embarked on a journey to find the source of the Nile River. Even though he was not able to find the final source but his journeys deep into Africa provided the possibility of new trade routes as well as facilitated culture exchange among people from the Mediterranean World and countries along the Nile.

Alexander's rule was not without violence and controversy. Although he was famous for his kindness to those who resisted peacefully but he was also brutal toward those who refused to submit to his authority. Cities who resisted him frequently had to endure mass murder and destruction to show the strength and determination of his regime.

Despite many victories the ambition of Alexander ultimately exceeded the capacity that his kingdom could offer. His vast conquests made his resources shaky and efforts to control the vast expanse of his empire was a challenge. The result was a rise in tension and discord between his officers and generals.

Alexander's death at age of 32 has been the subject of discussion and discussion.

There are theories that suggest his death was caused by poisoning, some suggest that it was due to the natural cause or a disease. The sudden death of his obvious successor left the creation of a power vacuum, and also an era of uncertainty that was referred to as The Wars of the Diadochi, in which his generals competed to control the empire he had built.

The interest in Alexander the Great is not just due to his victories in the military, but also because of his larger than life persona. Alexander became a cult figure across both Eastern as well as Western societies, inspiring many stories, novels as well as works of art. The legacy of his battle or visionary influencer continues to inspire and invigorate generations.

To conclude, Alexander the Great's biography illustrates a complicated and diverse person whose military accomplishments as well as his cultural and historical legacy still shape our knowledge of the past. His strategies, conquests and strategies left an irresistible impression on the territories which he conquered, and changed the history of civilisations throughout the centuries. Alexander's story is an example to his pursuit of excellence and the need for learning and the lasting influence of leadership that was visionary.

Infrastructure development

Alexander's campaign was not only focussed on the military's conquests. Alexander was also aware of the importance of infrastructure development as well as urban planning. He also embarked on massive construction initiatives, which included the establishment of new cities as well as the rehabilitation of old ones. The cities, dubbed Alexandrias were a symbol of his power and influence in addition to being centers of culture and trade.

Alongside his administrative and military pursuits, Alexander took a keen fascination with exploration and discovering. He was determined to discover the mysteries of the universe and to expand his knowledge of geography. He arranged expeditions in unknown territories, such as the discovery of the Caspian Sea and the mapping of the Indus River. This helped in an increase in understanding of geography in his time.

Alexander's close relationships with his most trusted group of friends, often referred to as his Companions or "Friends of Alexander," helped him achieve his goals. The dependable and trustworthy people, who knew him from when he was a child, created an internal circle of advisers and friends. Their loyalty and friendship was crucial to sustaining

Alexander's dreams and keeping the symbiosis of his army.

Through his various campaigns, Alexander encountered various cultures and civilizations with distinct traditions as well as languages and customs. In contrast to insisting on Greek cultural norms with force, he generally embraced a culture of culture assimilation. He encouraged exchanges of concepts, languages and traditions, leading to the fusion of many different cultures, and the expansion of Greek influence throughout vast regions.

Alexander's method of administration was marked with a mix of centralized power and autonomy for local authorities. Although the Satraps (governors) to supervise the running of his massive empire, he allowed local rulers to hold their power positions and abide by their local law and tradition. The balance of centralization and decentralization was instrumental in maintaining peace within the diverse territories of his empire.

Apart from his achievements in combat, Alexander also had a important influence in the development of thinking. The expansion of Greek culture as well as the development of Alexandrian educational centers led to the development of philosophical schools as well as the preservation of classic works. Philosophers and academics like Euclid, Archimedes, and Eratosthenes were able to make significant contributions at the time.

Alexander's influence on literature and art went on to influence literature and art for a long time beyond his own. The Hellenistic time that followed his reign saw an explosion in artistic expression. In this era, there was a rise of massive sculptures, elaborate mosaics and vivid paintings which reflected the cultural melting and variety in this Hellenistic world.

The passing of Alexander the Great was the beginning of an era as well as the start of a brand new chapter in the history of mankind. The huge empire that he constructed quickly fell apart, giving the birth of independent kingdoms as well as the emergence of power struggle between his commanders. The Hellenistic kingdoms which emerged following his demise, like the Ptolemaic Dynasty in Egypt as well as the Seleucid Empire of the east and carried on his legacy, while also establishing their own distinctive names.

The legacy that has remained from Alexander the Great is not just in his victories in the military, but through his influence on the expansion of Greek civilization, the growth in knowledge and mixing of different cultures. Alexander's vision, leadership and determination continue to excite and amaze people across the globe, making Alexander the

Great one of the most famous figures in the history of mankind.

The biography of Alexander the Great is an example of his incredible military skills as well as his cultural as well as his intellectual pursuits. Alexander's victories, his policies and influence changed the history of antiquity with a permanent mark on the territories that he conquered as well as the following generations. Alexander's journey through life is a fascinating adventure of exploration, ambition and the search for the highest level that has continued to capture our minds.

## Chapter 21: Determination

One of the main characteristics of Alexander's personality was his determination to fight for the highest good and unstoppable determination. He believed of his own fate and believed that he was an ordained leader who was destined to rule the globe. His unwavering faith in his own self-belief fuelled his drive and inspired him to face numerous difficulties and hurdles throughout his journey.

Alexander's military operations did not only involve combat with armies of enemies. Alexander also used diplomatic maneuvers and strategic diplomacy to establish alliances and eliminate the threat. Through clever negotiations and unions, he was able to strengthen his position and keep a equilibrium of influence between different nations and factions.

Apart from the military genius he displayed, Alexander possessed a charismatic and captivating personality, which attracted the soldiers to him and sparked the unstoppable loyalty of his troops. Alexander commanded at the front while fighting alongside his troops as they shared their struggles and triumphs. His bravery and courage during battle earned him the reverence and admiration from his troops.

Despite his incredible victory on the battlefield, Alexander was not without obstacles and setbacks in his battles. Alexander had to contend with formidable adversaries including the experienced Indian warrior Porus and his resistance, which tested his tactical savvy and leadership. Also, he was faced with the logistical difficulties, arid terrains and exhaustion of his soldiers as they embarked on lengthy and strenuous campaign.

Through his battles, Alexander exhibited a keen desire to integrate the different cultures of the nations which he defeated. Alexander sought to establish an environment of peace and co-operation by encouraging the acceptance of Greek culture, language, and practices. The cultural synthesis, referred to as Hellenization, made lasting and profound effects on the areas that he conquered, and influenced their architecture, art as well as their governance and academic endeavors over the course of centuries.

Alexander's private life did not come without its fair moments of conflict and tension. Alexander was in a turbulent relationships with his family members especially with his mother Olympias and father his king, Philip II of Macedon. There were conflicts and conspiracies within his own family, that led to exile, execution, or the assassination people who were threatening to his reign.

One of the oldest stories about Alexander is the story of his first encounter to his encounter with the Gordian Knot. According to the ancient stories that he stumbled upon an intricate knot knotted by the king Gordius of Phrygia and believed that the person who could cut the knot would be able to conquer Asia. With a daring move Alexander cut through the knot using the sword, showing the ability of his mind to think out of the boundaries and then take the decisive step.

Alexander's rise to fame ended with his premature passing away in 323 BC at 33 years old. There was no clear heir nor successor to the empire, it sank into a time of disintegration and civil conflicts. His conquests but, despite this, continues to influence the course of the world, impacting the development of empires that followed as well as leaving a permanent mark across the world.

In the end, the life of Alexander the Great is an enthralling story of leadership, ambition and military awe. Alexander's relentless pursuit of victory brilliant strategic thinking, his brilliance in strategy, as well as his influence on culture keep enthralling and inspiring generations. Alexander's reputation as a leader of vision, a cultural synthesizer, as well as famous figure in the history of the world continues to be a testament of his lasting legacy on the world's ancient history as well as the world beyond.

Empire expansion

In the course of Alexander increased his empire, he instituted policies for stimulating cultural exchange as well as intellectual development. He set up institutions, like that of the Library of Alexandria, which has become one of the top research centers throughout the world. It housed many thousands of scrolls. It also attracted researchers from a variety of disciplines. It contributed to the progress of philosophy, science, and the study of literature.

Alexander's life as a person was characterized by a variety of relationships as well as romantic relationships. He was married multiple times, forming relationships with the state through marriages strategically planned. The most well-known marriage was that of Roxana who was a Bactrian princess who had the name of Alexander IV. But tensions in his court and conflicts of loyalty to his family sometimes caused tension in his relations and led to incidents of resentment and political intrigue.

Although he was a military man, Alexander recognized the importance of commerce and economic development. Alexander encouraged commerce and erected new trade routes linking all the regions within his empire. They allowed for the exchange of ideas, goods as well as cultural influences encouraging economic growth as well as diversification of culture.

Alexander's victories had an enormous influence on architecture and art. The merging of Greek and regional styles of art led to the creation of the unique Hellenistic art style. Massive sculptures, elaborate mosaics, and magnificent constructions adorned cities of his empire and showcased his artistic accomplishments during the time.

Alexander's passion for exploring and discovering extended far beyond the boundaries of his military expeditions. Alexander was fascinated by the undiscovered and aspired to expand the limits of our understanding. He led expeditions to investigate the deepest parts of the Arabian Desert, the remote areas in the Hindu Kush, and the famous Mount Olympus. These expeditions fuelled his interest and helped him gain a better knowledge of the world.

In all his years, Alexander displayed a deep reverence and respect of Greek mythology and culture. He believed that he was an ancestor of the early Greek heroes, and sought to imitate their feats of courage. He favored poets - playswrights, philosophers, and playwrights helping to develop Greek writing and thinking during his time.

Alongside his accomplishments in military and the arts, Alexander was known for his athleticism and physical strength. Alexander competed in a variety of sports as well as being a keen horse rider. The horse he favored, Bucephalus, became legendary due to its bravery and loyalty and mirrored Alexander's qualities.

In the final years of his reign, Alexander's goals became more extravagant. He set off on a quest to besiege all of Arabian Peninsula and explore the west coast of the Mediterranean. But his tragic death in Babylon put an end to these plans which left many unanswered questions on how much more he could achieve.

The influence of Alexander the Great endured for a long time after the death of his son The empire, although short-lived but left an impression across the globe. The spreading of Greek languages, cultures, as well as ideas, shaped the Hellenistic period, which influenced the sciences, arts, as well as the political system of the Mediterranean as well as in the Near East.

www.ingramcontent.com/pod-product-compliance
Lightning Source LLC
Chambersburg PA
CBHW071439080526
44587CB00014B/1914